Igor Sukhin

Chess Camp

Volume 6: Tactics in Attack and Defense

MONGOOSE
Press

Publisher: Mongoose Press
1005 Boylston Street, Suite 324
Newton Highlands, MA 02461
info@mongoosepress.com
www.MongoosePress.com
ISBN: 978-1-936277-29-2 1-936277-29-8
Library of Congress Control Number: 2010932524
Distributed to the trade by National Book Network
custserv@nbnbooks.com, 800-462-6420
For all other sales inquiries please contact the publisher.

Editor: Jorge Amador
Typesetting: Frisco Del Rosario
Cover Design: Al Dianov
First English edition
0 987654321

Contents

Tactics in the Attack

Winning the Queen

Winning a Rook

Winning a Bishop

Winning a Knight

Defensive Tactics

Practice

Solutions

Note for Coaches, Parents, Teachers, and Trainers

This book of chess problems challenges the student to practice typical tactical ideas. There is a great number of such motifs in both attack and defense. Some of these ideas – including the "cross" (a type of double pin), the unstoppable attack, closing the trap, the skewer, the x-ray attack, removing the guard, reinforcing the attack, and many others – are not always given the kind of attention they deserve.

Many books cover typical attacking methods, but very few provide adequate coverage of defensive techniques. This can be explained from a psychological standpoint: it is more exciting to look for winning moves than it is to try to defend a bad position. However, in order to become a great player, the student needs to know how to both attack and defend. That is why learning typical defensive methods is no less important than knowing attacking methods.

Learning the typical ways to defend is not easy. Therefore, in this book most problems are arranged by topic, which will serve as a hint for the student. The next volume in this series, however, will offer problems with no hints, so as to reinforce the skills acquired while reading this book.

To become a great player, the student needs to learn both skills: how to attack and how to defend.

Winning the Queen

Giving check to win the queen

Skewer check

Black to move.

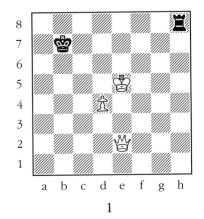

1

2

3

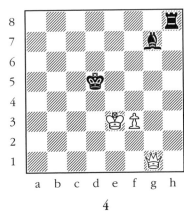

4

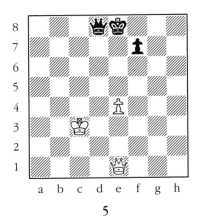

5

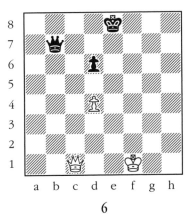

6

Remove the guard

White to move.

7

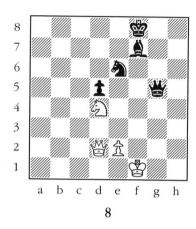

8

9

10

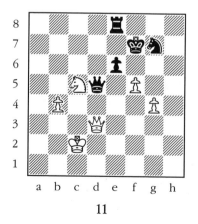

11

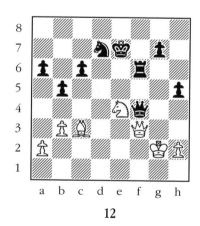

12

8

Double attack

White to move.

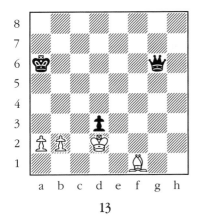

13

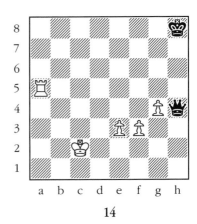

14

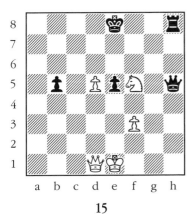

15

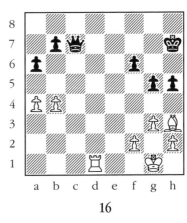

16

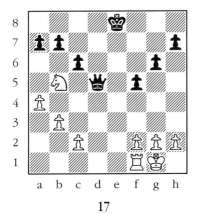

17

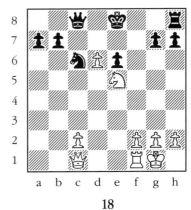

18

Double check

White to move.

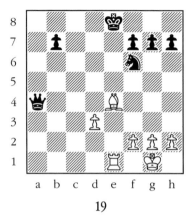

19

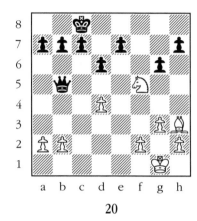

20

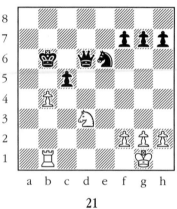

21

22

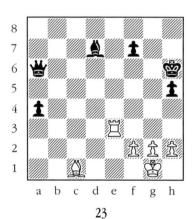

23

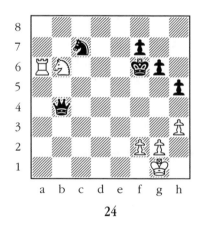

24

Discovered check

White to move.

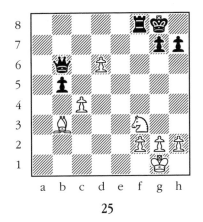

25

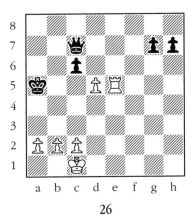

26

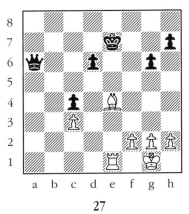

27

28

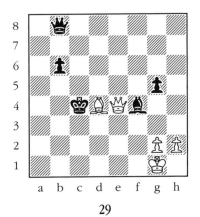

29

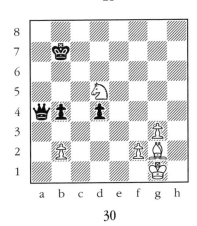

30

Discovered attack

White to move.

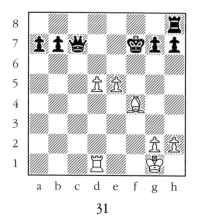

31

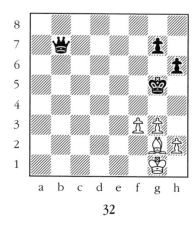

32

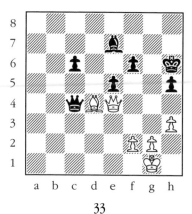

33

34

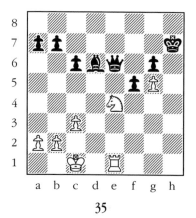

35

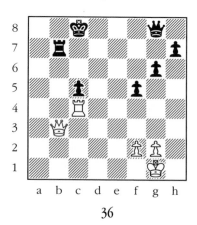

36

Give a check that forces Black
to sacrifice the queen

White to move.

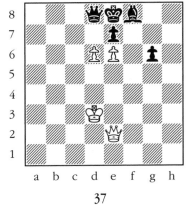

37

38

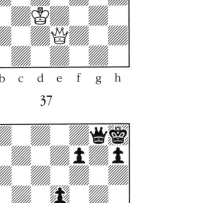

39

40

41

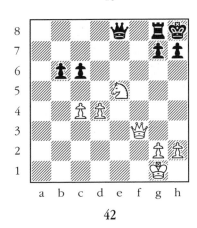

42

Deflect the white king from defending the queen

Black to move.

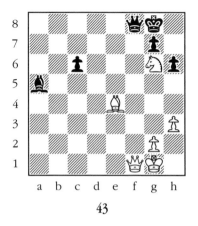

43

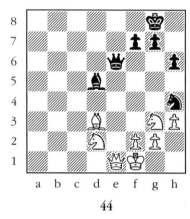

44

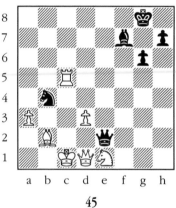

45

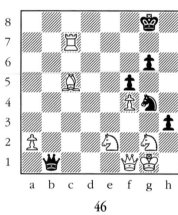

46

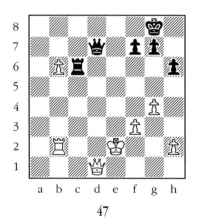

47

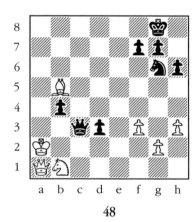

48

Deflect the black king from defending the queen

White to move.

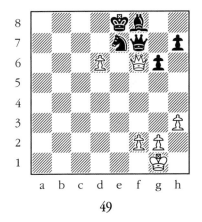

49

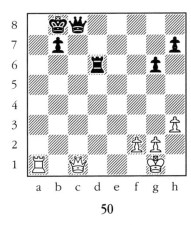

50

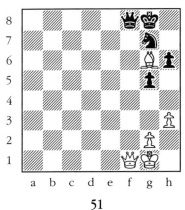

51

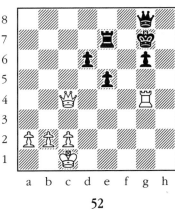

52

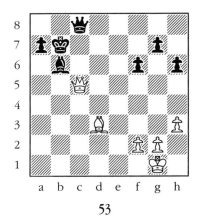

53

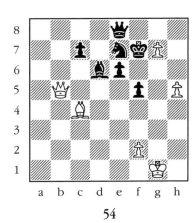

54

Sacrifice to set up a skewer

White to move.

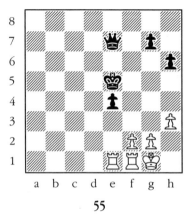

55

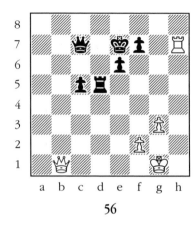

56

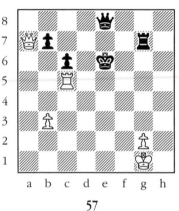

57

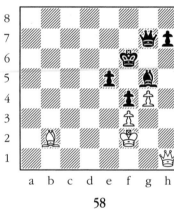

58

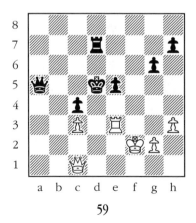

59

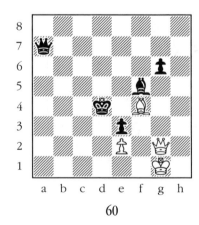

60

Sacrifice to set up a double attack

White to move.

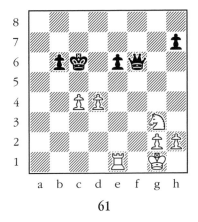

61

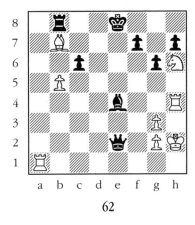

62

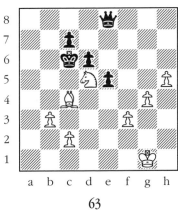

63

64

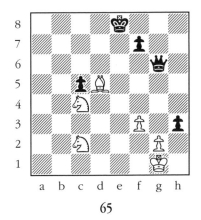

65

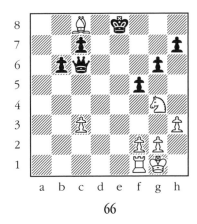

66

X-ray attack

Black to move.

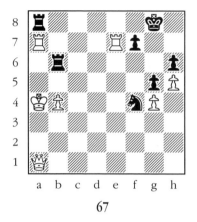

67

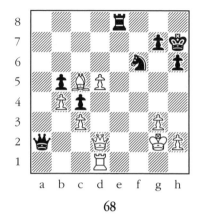

68

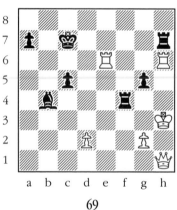

69

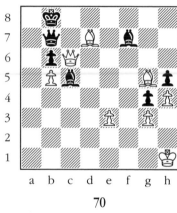

70

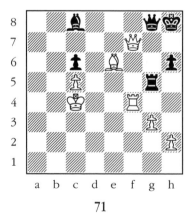

71

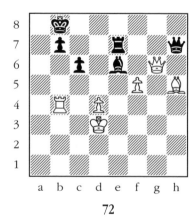

72

18

Exploit a pinned chessman

White to move.

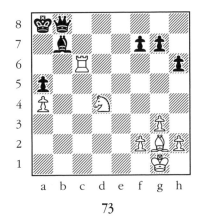

73

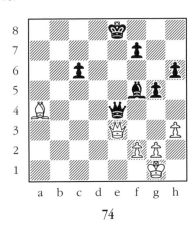

74

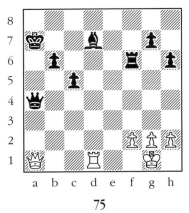

75

76

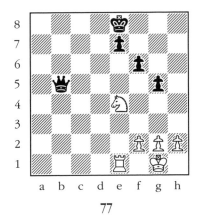

77

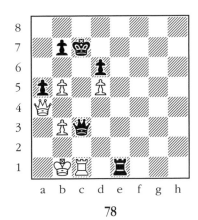

78

19

Sacrifice to create a pin

Black to move.

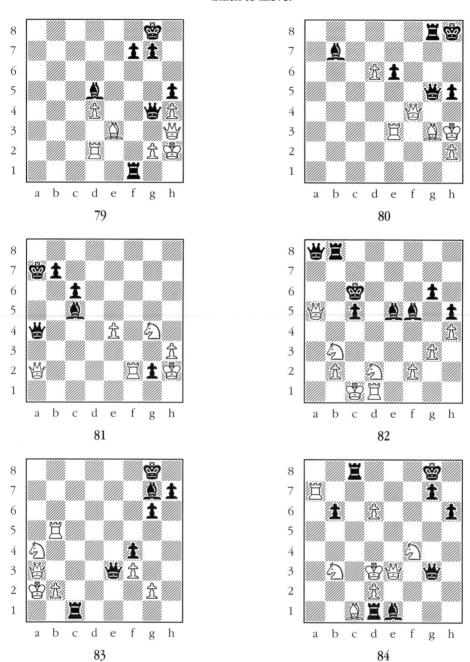

79

80

81

82

83

84

Force Black into a pin

White to move.

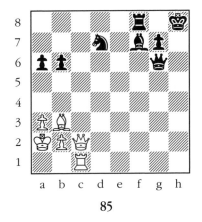

85

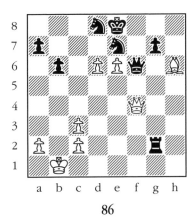

86

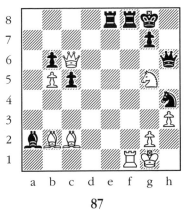

87

88

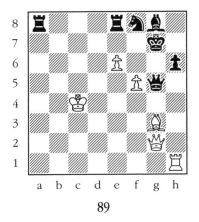

89

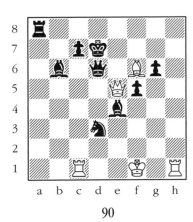

90

Two checks in a row

White to move.

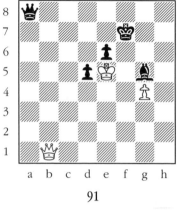

91

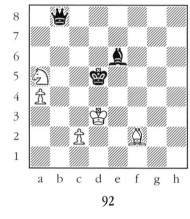

92

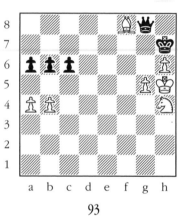

93

94

95

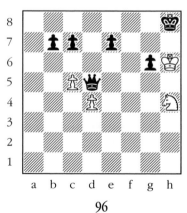

96

Winning the queen without giving check on the first move

Trap the queen

White to move.

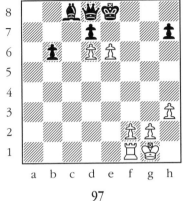

97

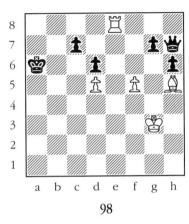

98

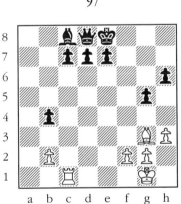

99

100

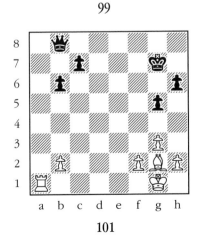

101

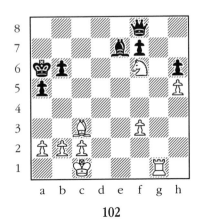

102

23

Double attack on the queen

Black to move.

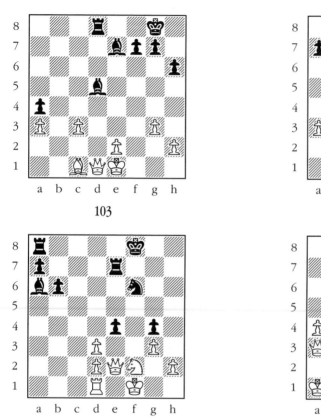

103

104

105

106

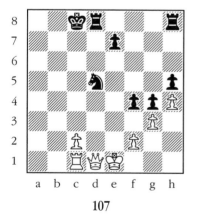

107

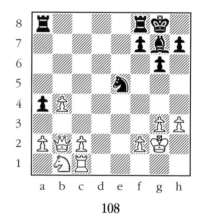

108

Zugzwang

White to move.

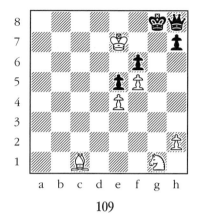

109

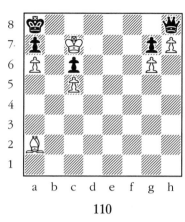

110

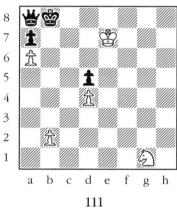

111

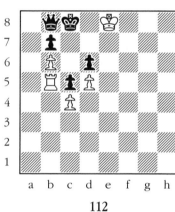

112

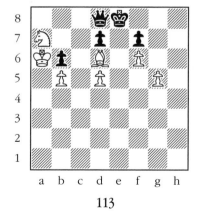

113

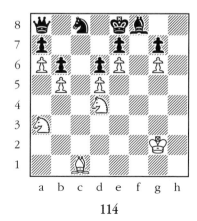

114

25

Pin the white queen to the white king

Black to move.

115

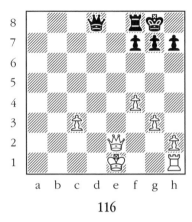

116

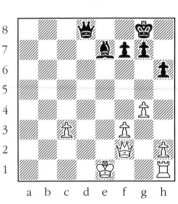

117

118

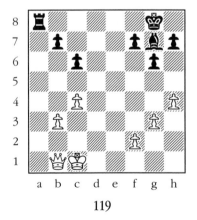

119

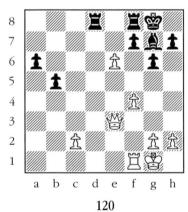

120

Pin followed by double attack

White to move.

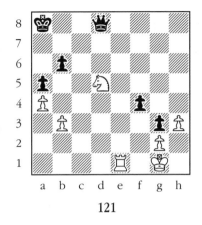

121

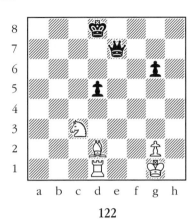

122

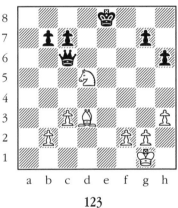

123

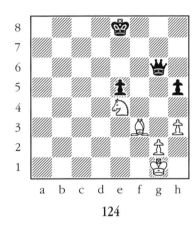

124

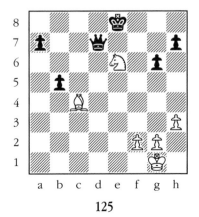

125

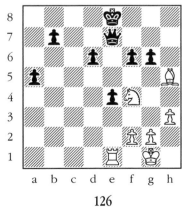

126

Pawn promotion

White to move.

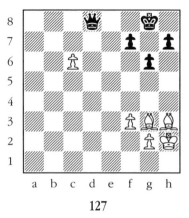

127

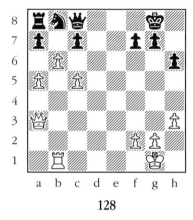

128

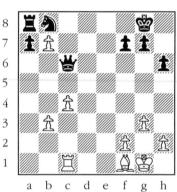

129

130

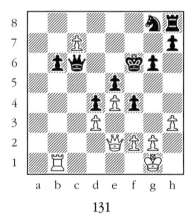

131

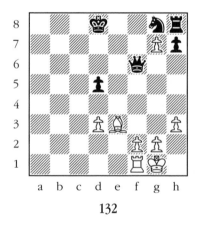

132

Threaten checkmate

White to move.

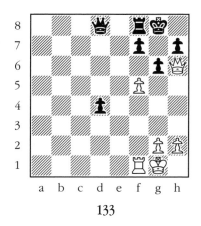

133

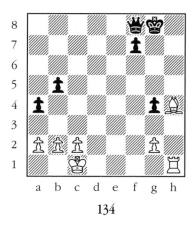

134

135

136

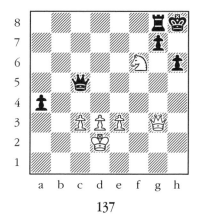

137

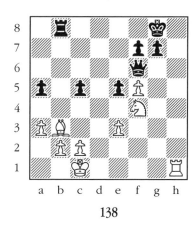

138

29

Winning a Rook

Skewer check to win a rook

Black to move.

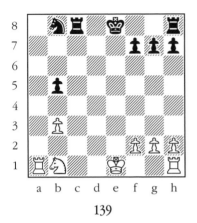

139

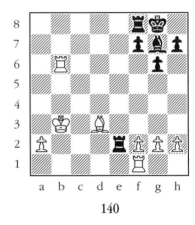

140

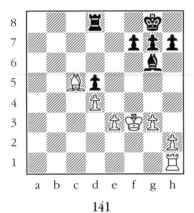

141

142

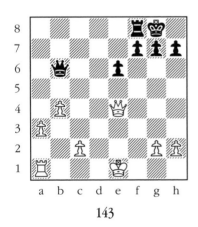

143

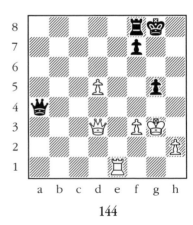

144

Remove the guard

White to move.

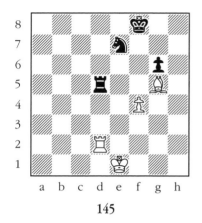

145

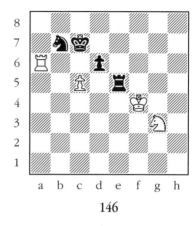

146

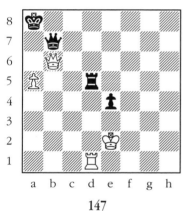

147

148

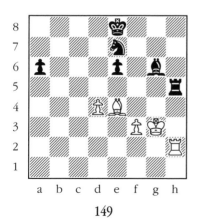

149

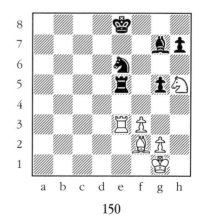

150

Double attack

White to move.

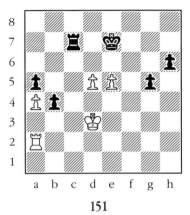

151

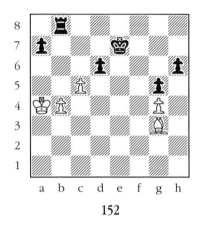

152

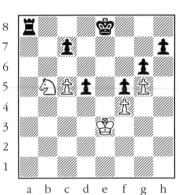

153

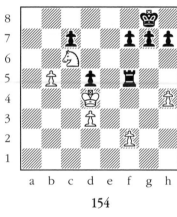

154

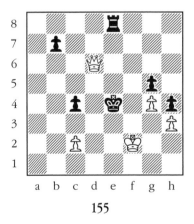

155

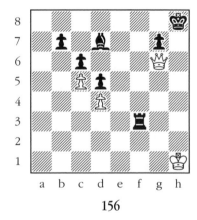

156

Double check

Black to move.

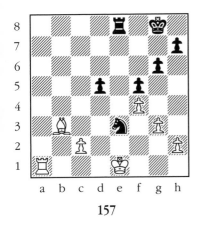

157

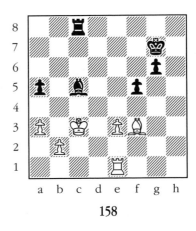

158

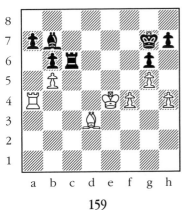

159

160

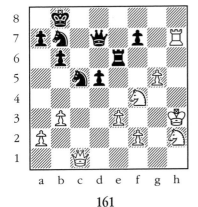

161

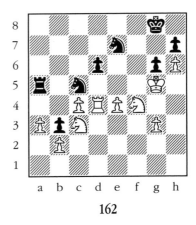

162

Discovered check

Black to move.

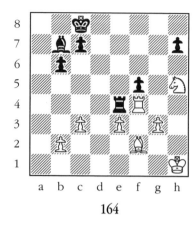

163

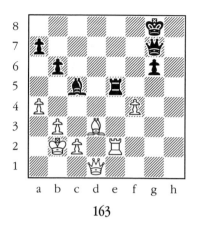

164

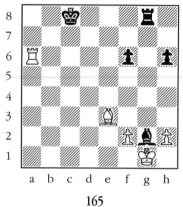

165

166

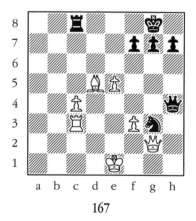

167

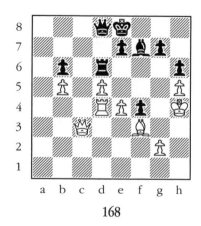

168

Discovered attack

White to move.

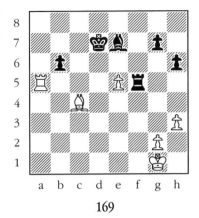

169

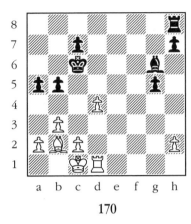

170

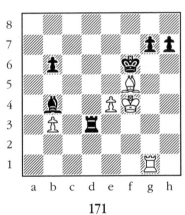

171

172

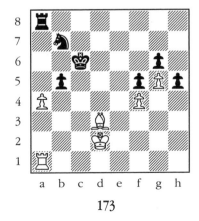

173

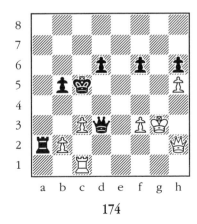

174

Give a check that forces Black
to sacrifice the rook

White to move.

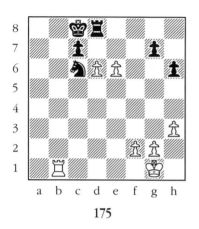

175

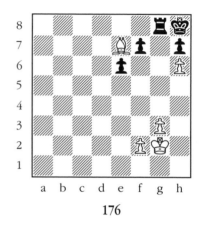

176

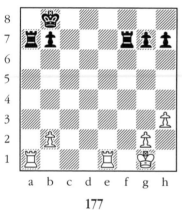

177

178

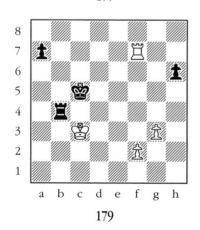

179

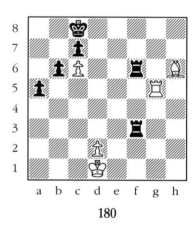

180

36

Deflect the king

White to move.

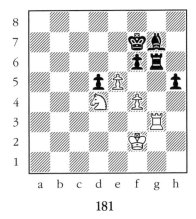

181

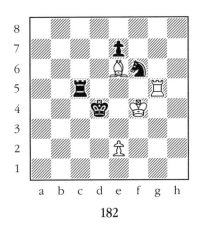

182

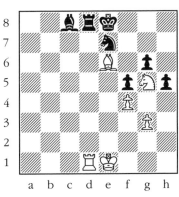

183

184

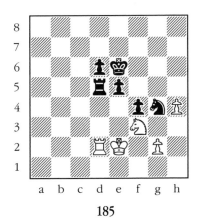

185

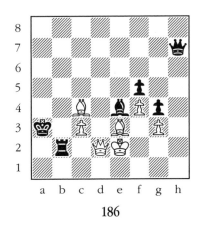

186

37

Exploit a pinned chessman

White to move.

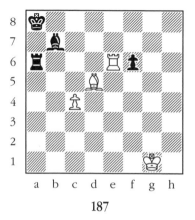

187

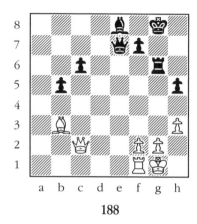

188

189

190

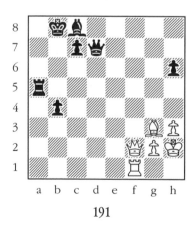

191

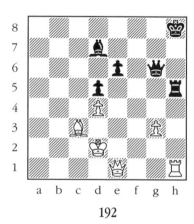

192

Reinforce the attack

Black to move.

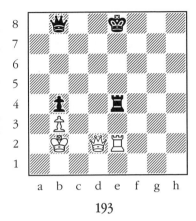

193

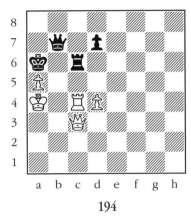

194

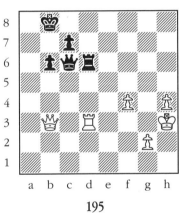

195

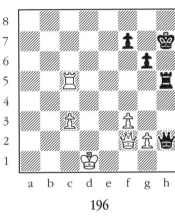

196

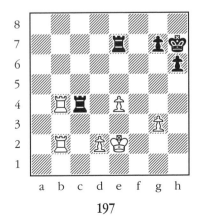

197

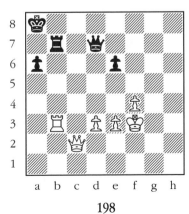

198

Two checks in a row

White to move.

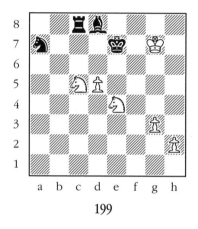

199

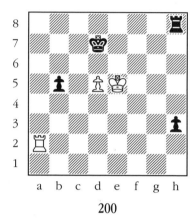

200

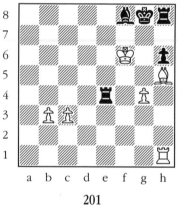

201

202

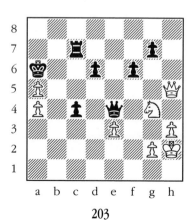

203

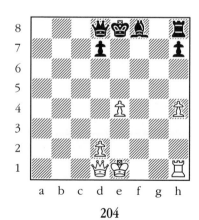

204

40

Winning a rook without giving check on the first move

Trap the rook

White to move.

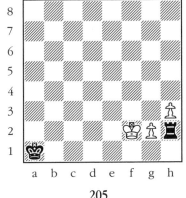

205

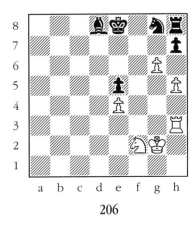

206

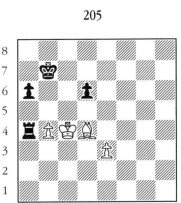

207

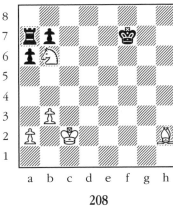

208

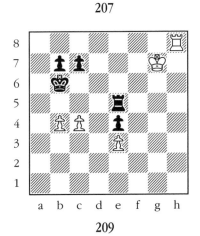

209

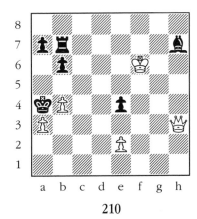

210

Skewer

Black to move.

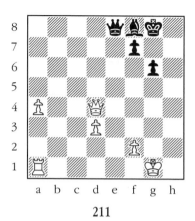

211

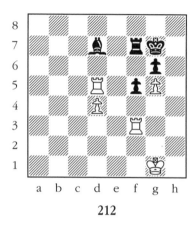

212

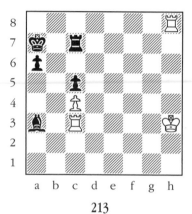

213

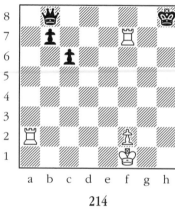

214

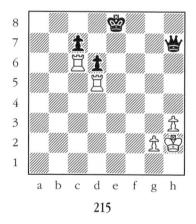

215

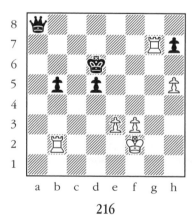

216

Remove the guard

Black to move.

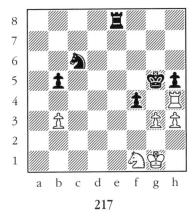

217

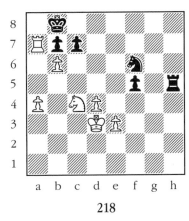

218

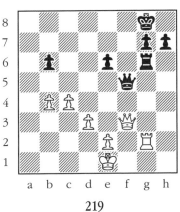

219

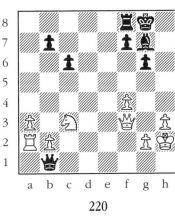

220

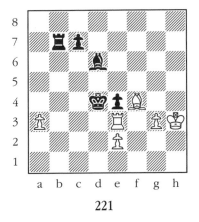

221

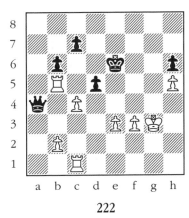

222

Double attack

White to move.

223

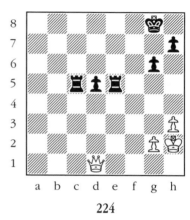

224

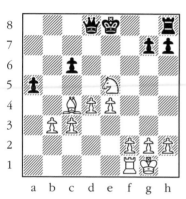

225

226

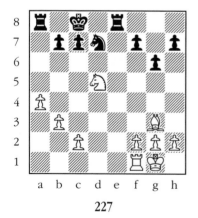

227

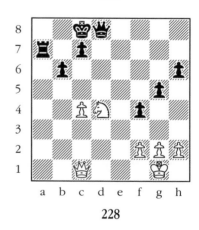

228

Discovered attack

Black to move.

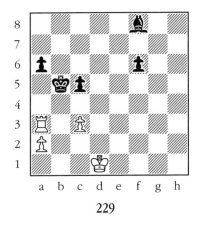

229

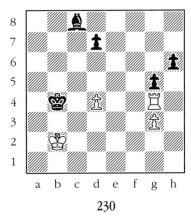

230

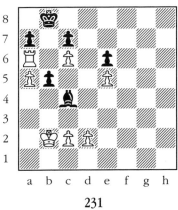

231

232

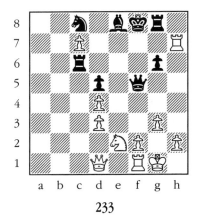

233

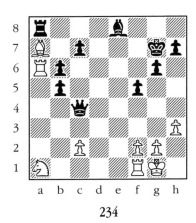

234

Attack the defender

Black to move.

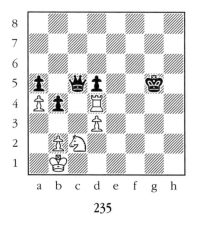

235

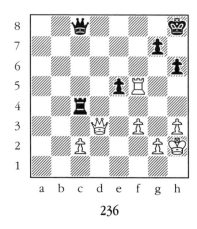

236

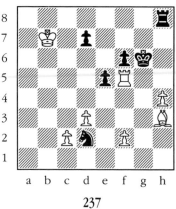

237

238

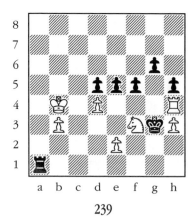

239

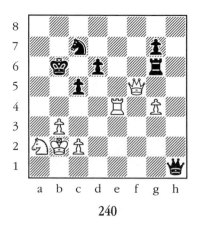

240

Zugzwang

White to move.

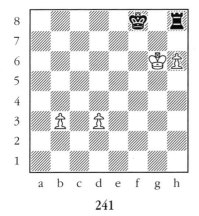

241

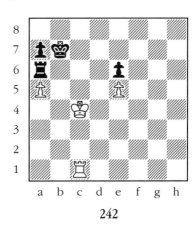

242

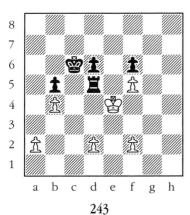

243

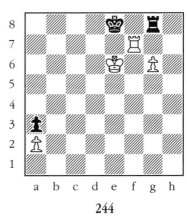

244

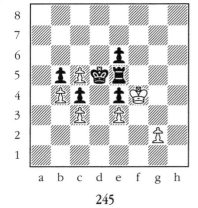

245

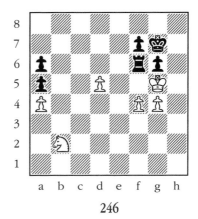

246

47

Close the trap

Black to move.

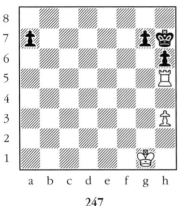

247

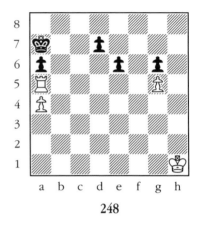

248

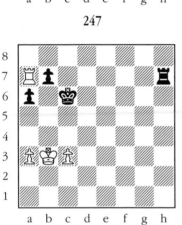

249

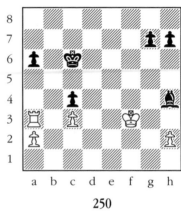

250

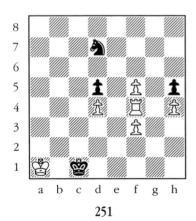

251

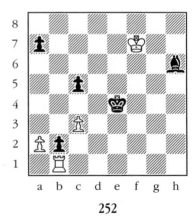

252

Pin

Black to move.

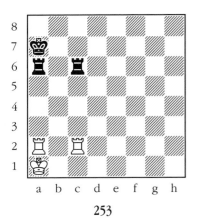

253

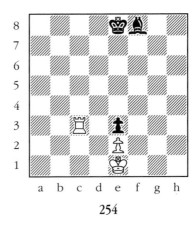

254

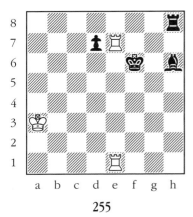

255

256

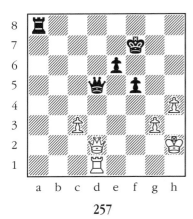

257

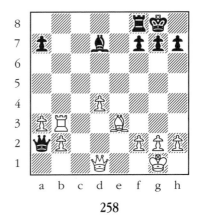

258

The cross-pin

Win a rook or get a queen for a rook

White to move.

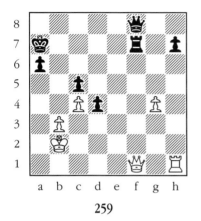

259

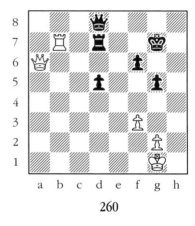

260

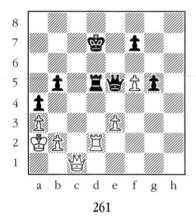

261

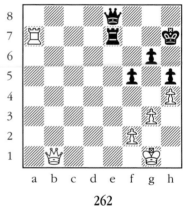

262

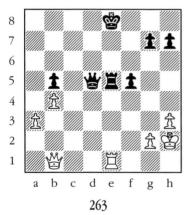

263

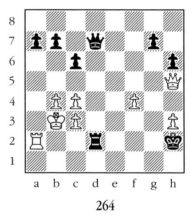

264

Mate threat

Black to move.

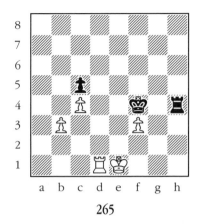

265

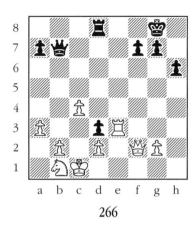

266

267

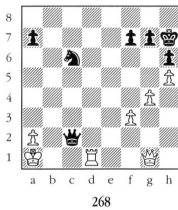

268

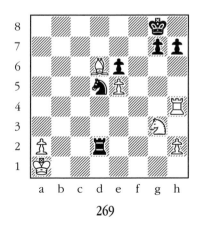

269

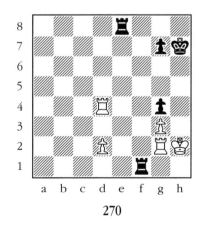

270

Winning a Bishop
Giving check to win a bishop
Skewer check
Black to move.

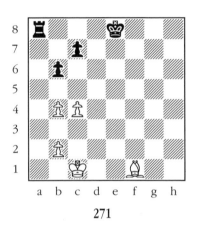

271

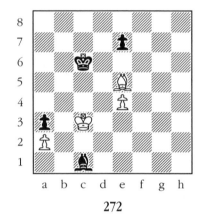

272

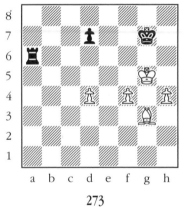

273

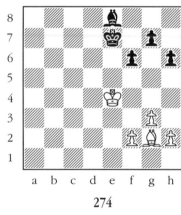

274

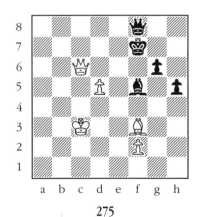

275

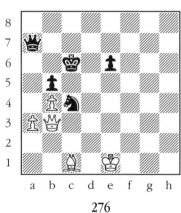

276

Remove the guard

White to move.

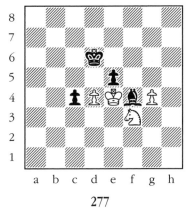

277

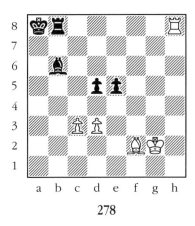

278

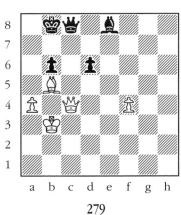

279

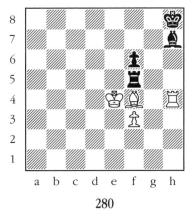

280

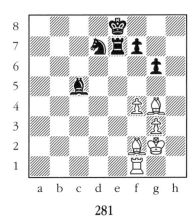

281

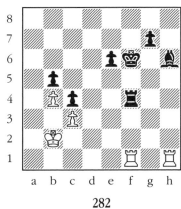

282

Double attack

White to move.

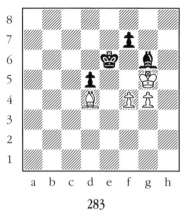

283

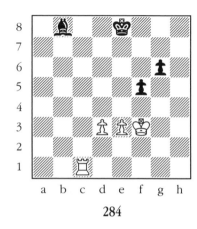

284

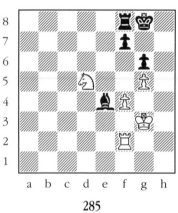

285

286

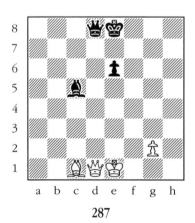

287

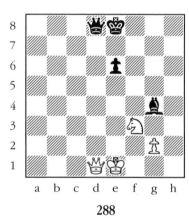

288

Double check

Black to move.

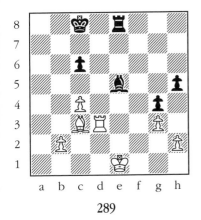

289

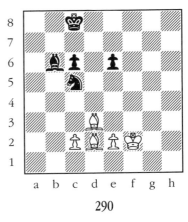

290

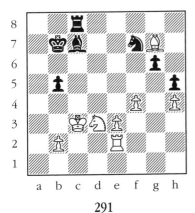

291

292

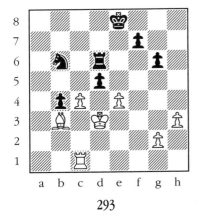

293

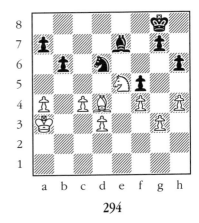

294

Discovered check

White to move.

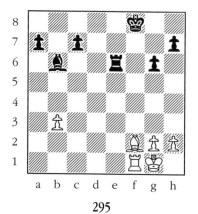

295

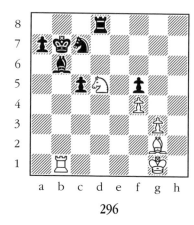

296

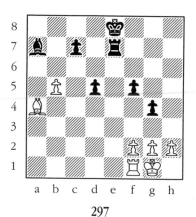

297

298

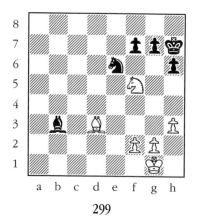

299

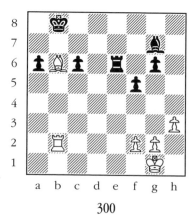

300

Discovered attack

Black to move.

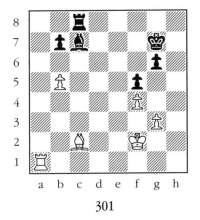

301

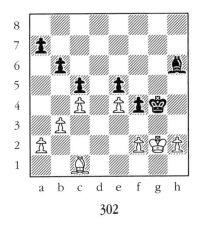

302

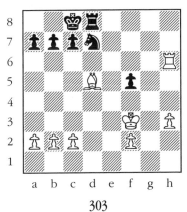

303

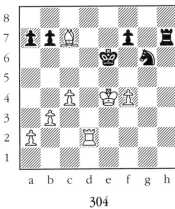

304

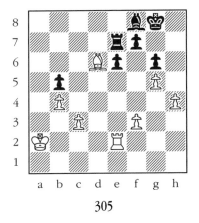

305

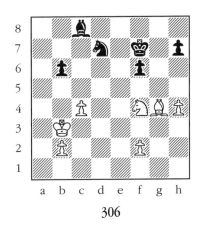

306

Give a check that forces White to sacrifice the bishop

Black to move.

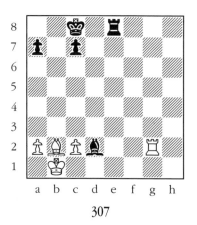

307

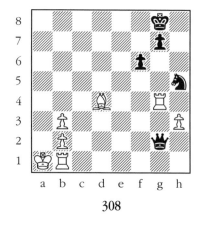

308

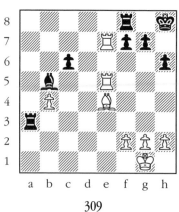

309

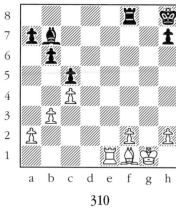

310

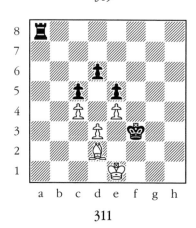

311

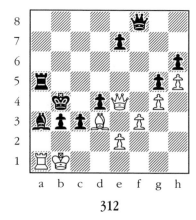

312

58

Pin

White to move.

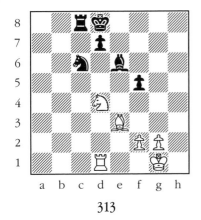

313

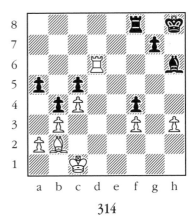

314

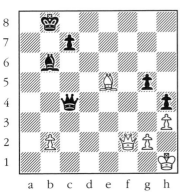

315

316

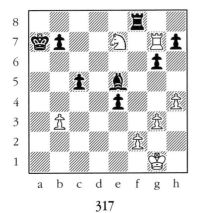

317

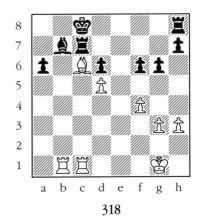

318

Reinforce the attack

White to move.

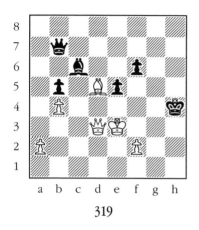

319

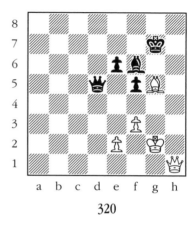

320

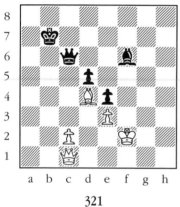

321

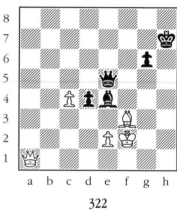

322

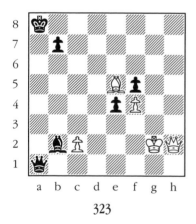

323

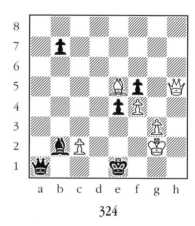

324

Give two checks in a row to win the bishop

White to move.

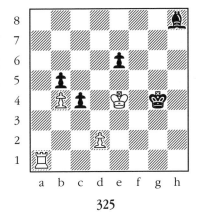

325

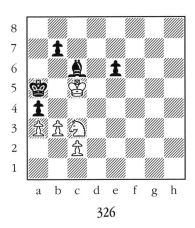

326

327

328

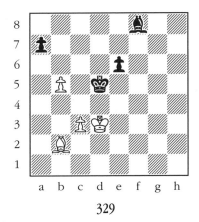

329

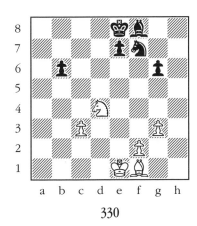

330

Winning a bishop without giving check on the first move
Trap the bishop

Black to move.

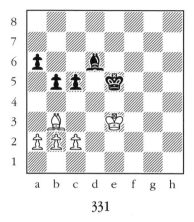

331

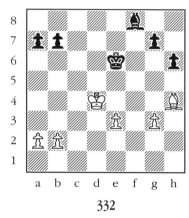

332

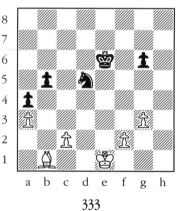

333

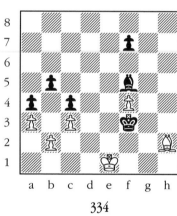

334

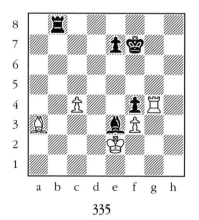

335

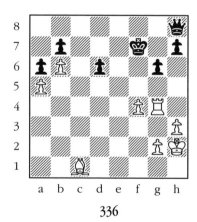

336

Skewer

White to move.

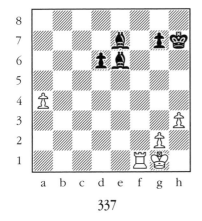

337

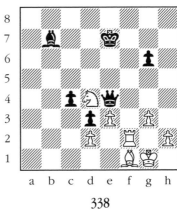

338

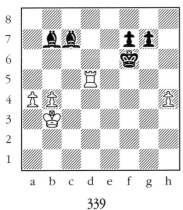

339

340

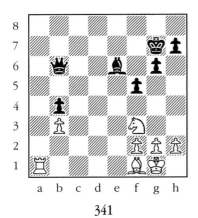

341

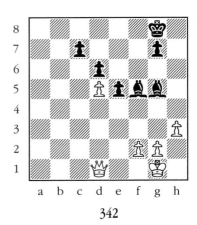

342

Double attack

White to move.

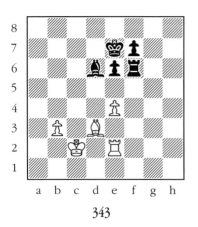

343

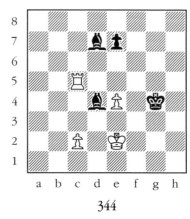

344

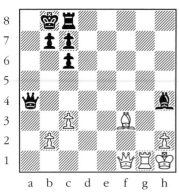

345

346

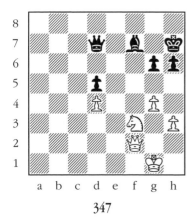

347

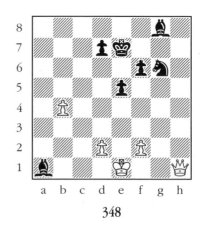

348

Attack the defender

White to move.

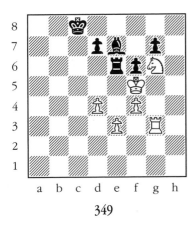

349

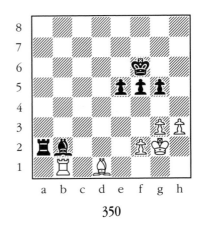

350

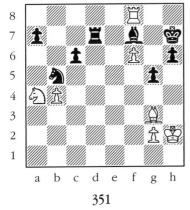

351

352

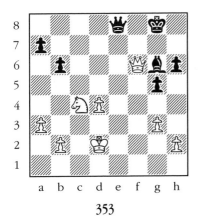

353

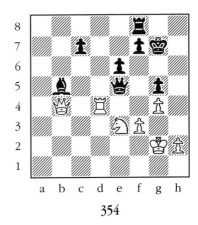

354

Zugzwang

Black to move.

355

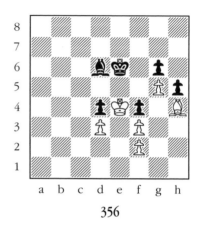

356

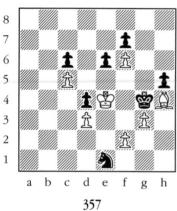

357

358

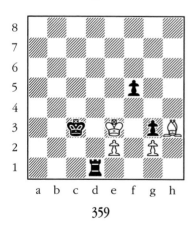

359

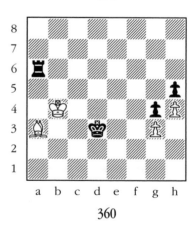

360

Close the trap

White to move.

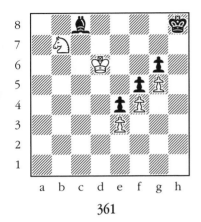

361

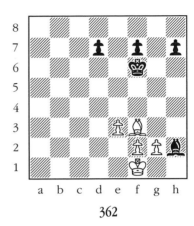

362

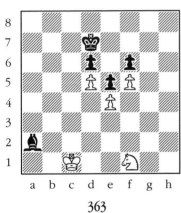

363

364

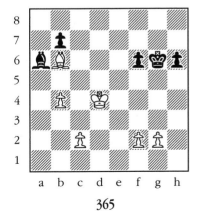

365

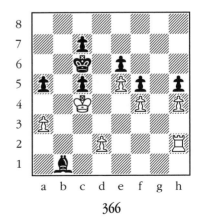

366

Pin

White to move.

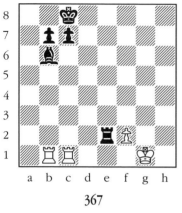

367

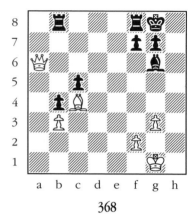

368

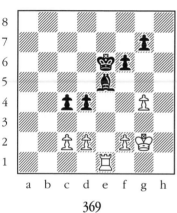

369

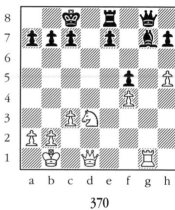

370

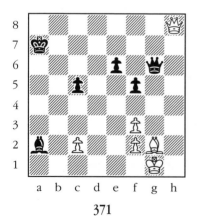

371

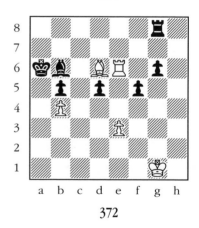

372

The cross-pin

White to move.

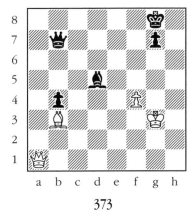

373

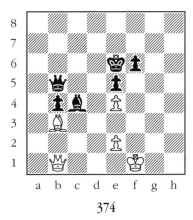

374

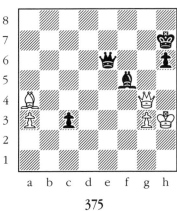

375

376

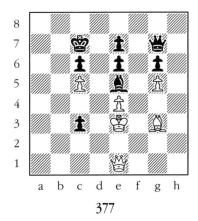

377

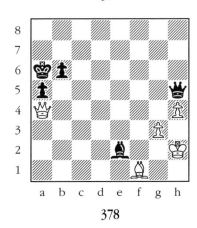

378

Winning a Knight
Giving check to win a knight
Skewer check

White to move.

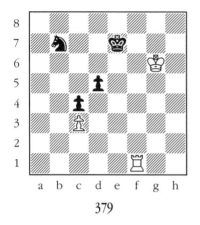

379

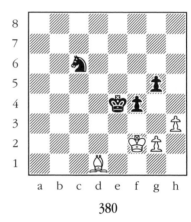

380

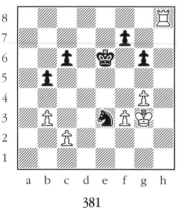

381

382

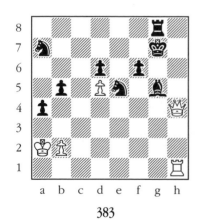

383

384

Remove the guard

Black to move.

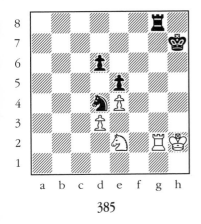

385

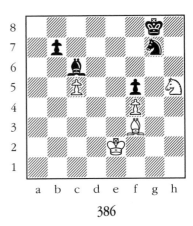

386

387

388

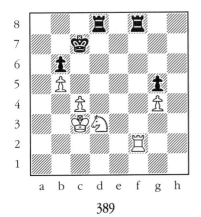

389

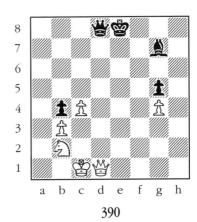

390

Double attack

White to move.

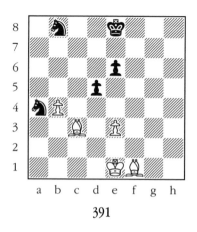

391

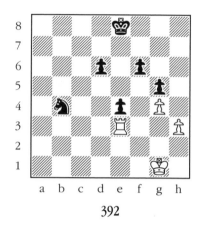

392

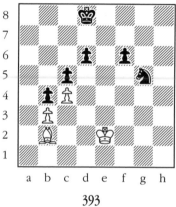

393

394

395

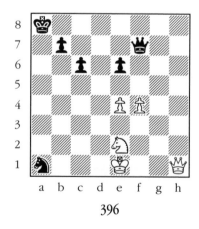

396

Discovered check

Black to move.

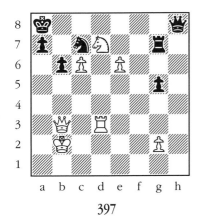

397

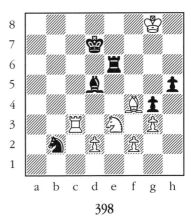

398

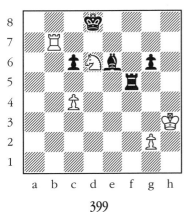

399

400

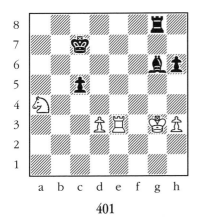

401

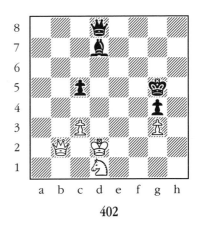

402

73

Discovered attack

White to move.

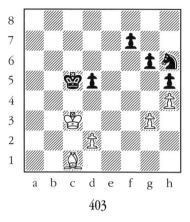

403

404

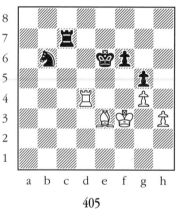

405

406

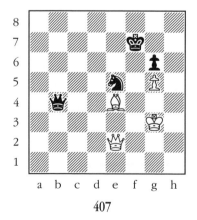

407

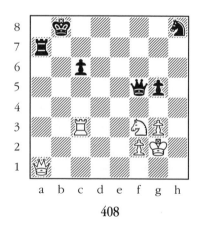

408

Give a check that forces Black
to sacrifice the knight

White to move.

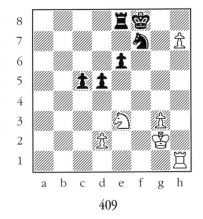

409

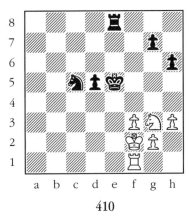

410

411

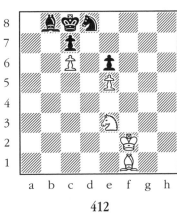

412

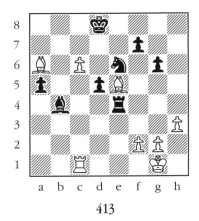

413

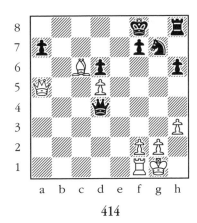

414

Pin

Black to move.

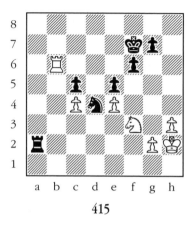

415

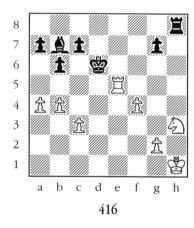

416

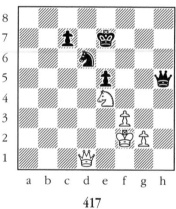

417

418

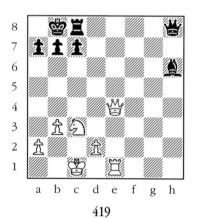

419

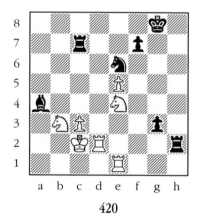

420

Winning a knight without giving check on the first move
Trap the knight

White to move.

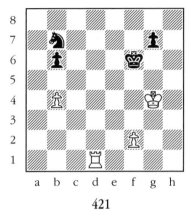

421

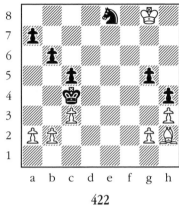

422

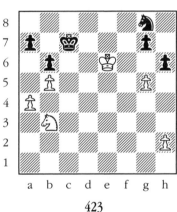

423

424

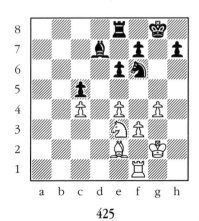

425

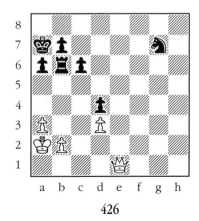

426

Skewer

Black to move.

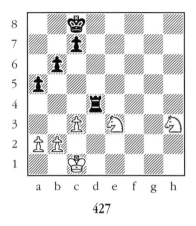

427

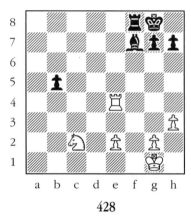

428

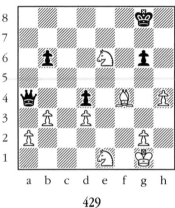

429

430

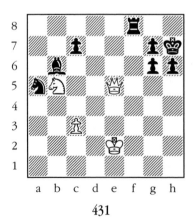

431

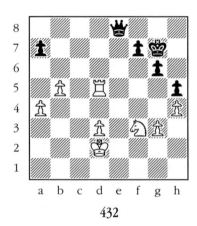

432

Double attack

Black to move.

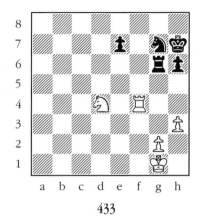

433

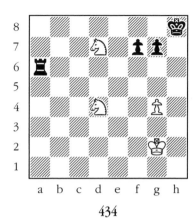

434

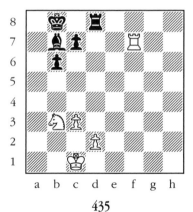

435

436

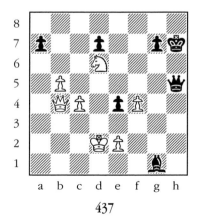

437

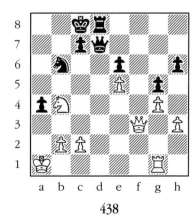

438

Attack the defender

Black to move.

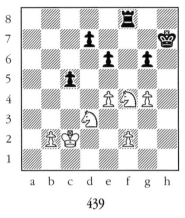

439

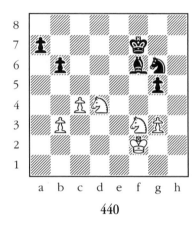

440

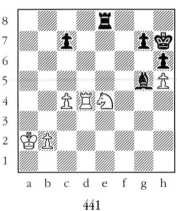

441

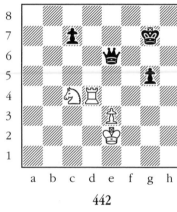

442

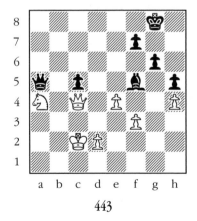

443

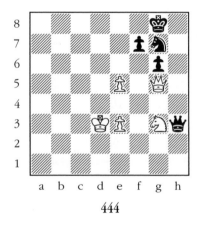

444

Close the trap

Black to move.

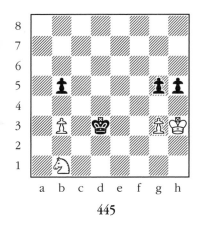

445

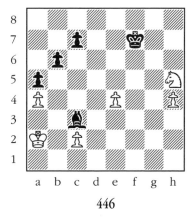

446

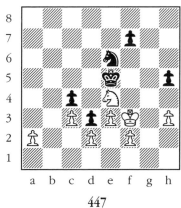

447

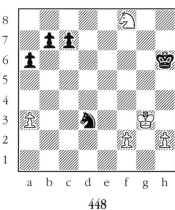

448

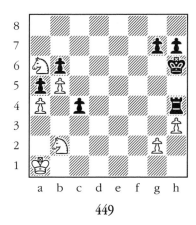

449

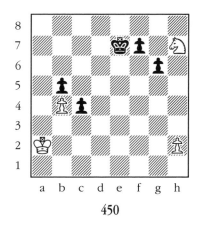

450

Pin

Black to move.

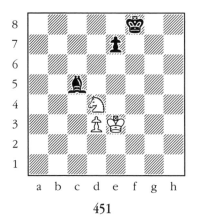

451

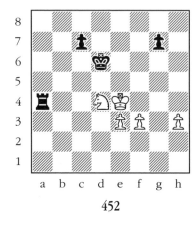

452

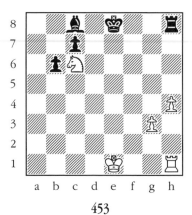

453

454

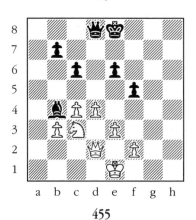

455

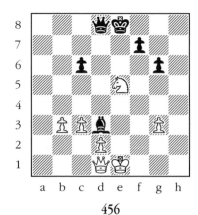

456

Defensive Tactics
Saving the king
Eliminate the attacker

Black to move.

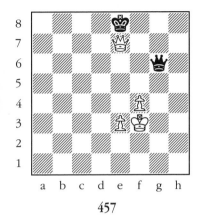

457

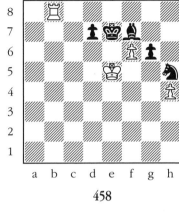

458

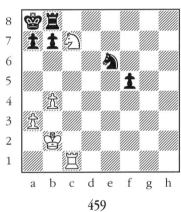

459

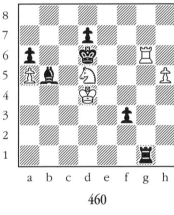

460

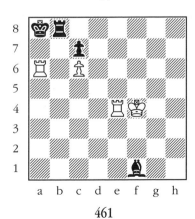

461

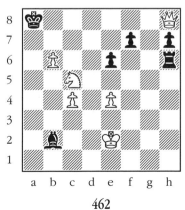

462

Get away from the attacked square

White to move.

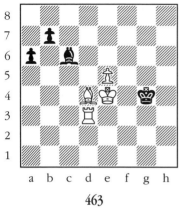

463

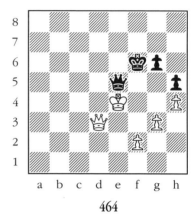

464

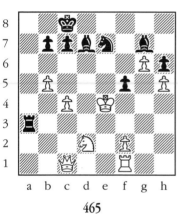

465

466

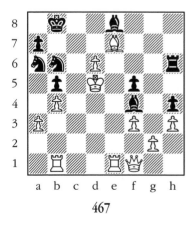

467

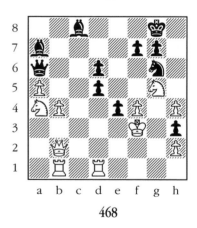

468

Block the check by interposing a piece or pawn

White to move.

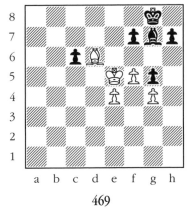

469

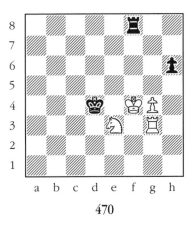

470

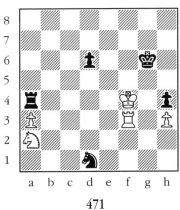

471

472

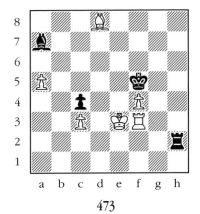

473

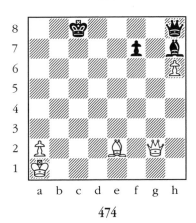

474

Find the best defense

Black to move.

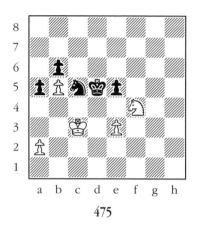

475

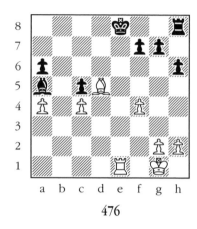

476

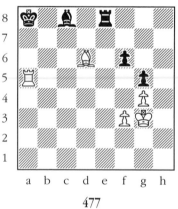

477

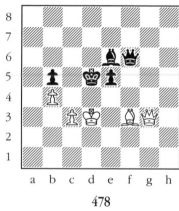

478

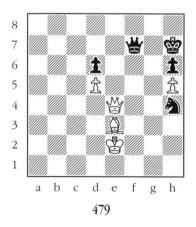

479

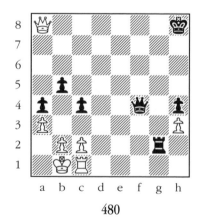

480

Saving the queen
Eliminate the attacker

White to move.

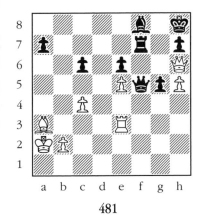

481

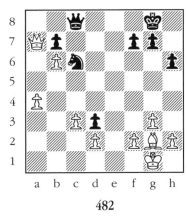

482

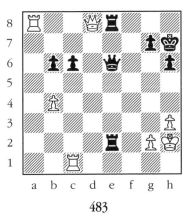

483

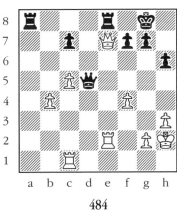

484

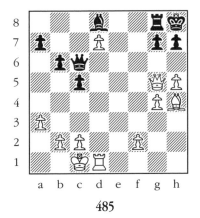

485

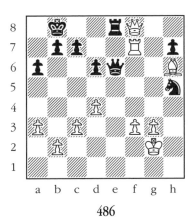

486

Get away from the attacked square

White to move.

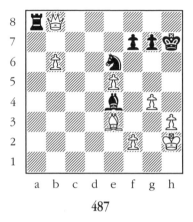

487

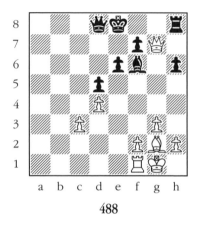

488

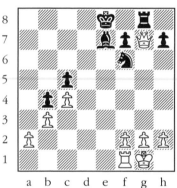

489

490

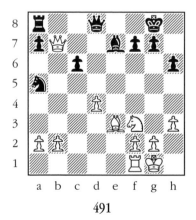

491

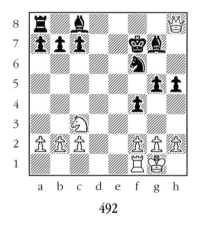

492

Block the attack on the queen

Black to move.

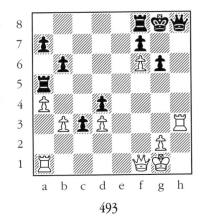

493

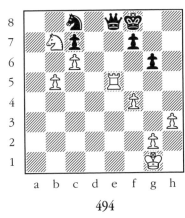

494

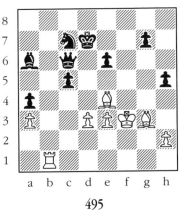

495

496

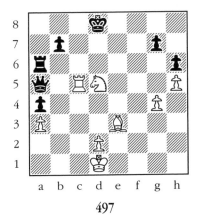

497

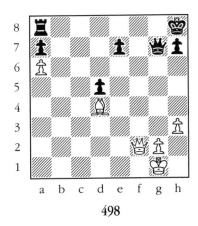

498

Counterattack

Black to move.

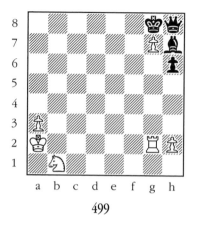

499

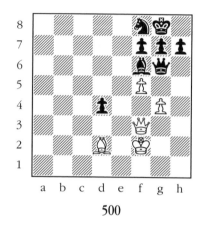

500

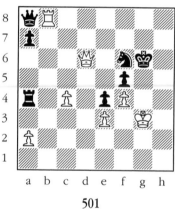

501

502

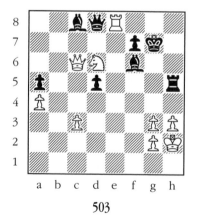

503

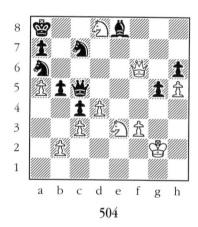

504

Stalemate

White to move.

505

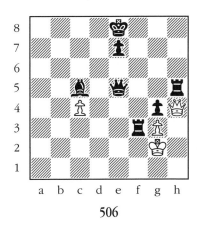

506

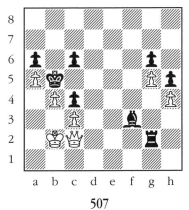

507

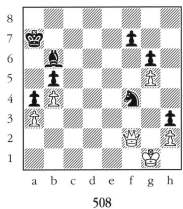

508

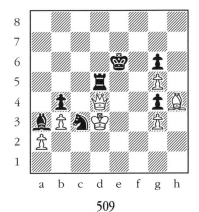

509

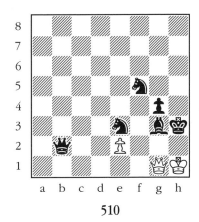

510

Perpetual check

Black to move.

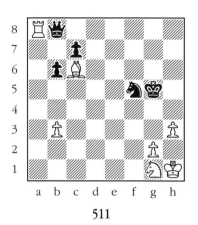

511

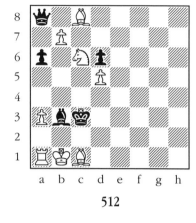

512

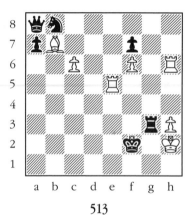

513

514

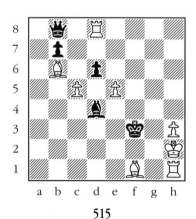

515

516

Pin

White to move.

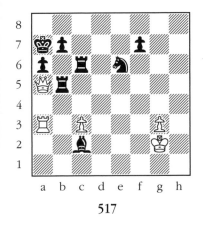

517

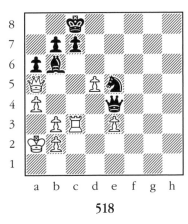

518

519

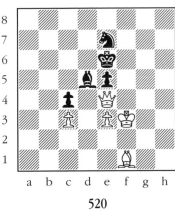

520

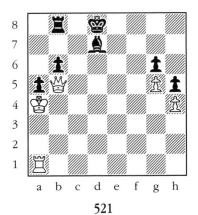

521

522

Mate threat

White to move.

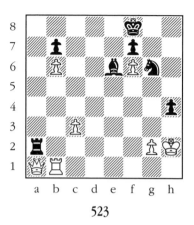

523

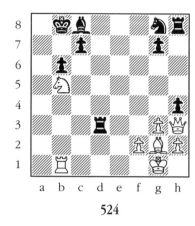

524

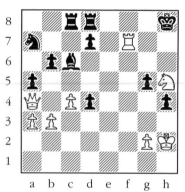

525

526

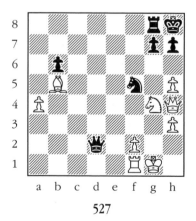

527

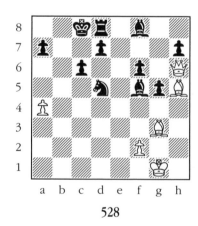

528

Saving a rook

Evacuate the attacked square

Black to move.

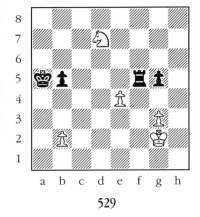

529

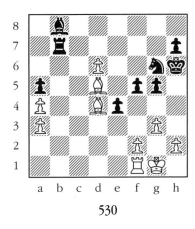

530

531

532

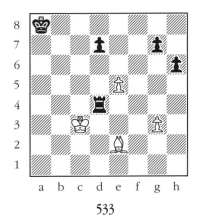

533

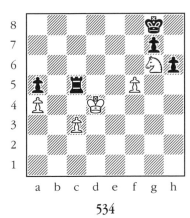

534

Interpose

White to move.

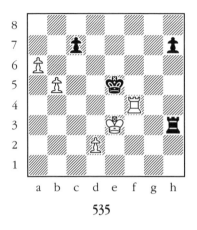

535

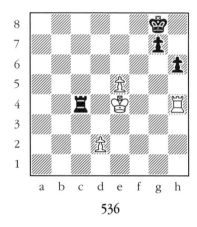

536

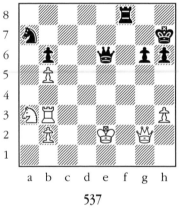

537

538

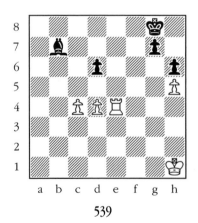

539

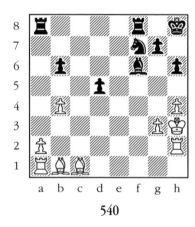

540

Counterattack

Black to move.

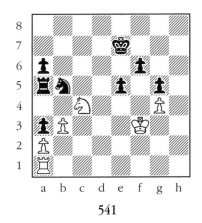

541

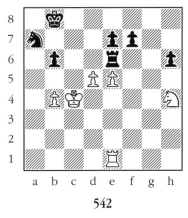

542

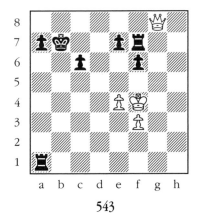

543

544

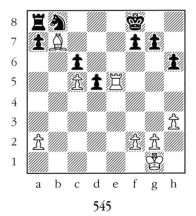

545

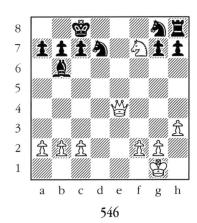

546

Defend with another piece

Black to move.

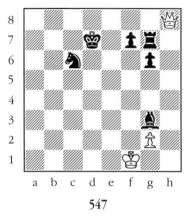

547

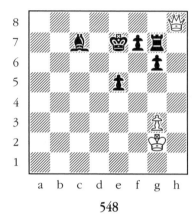

548

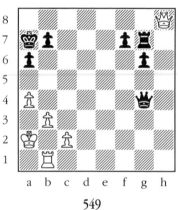

549

550

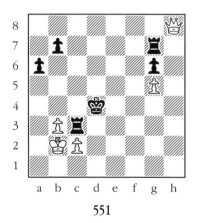

551

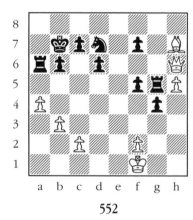

552

Pin

White to move.

553

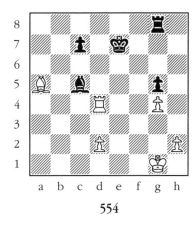

554

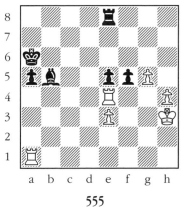

555

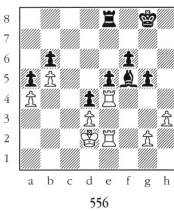

556

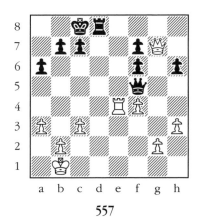

557

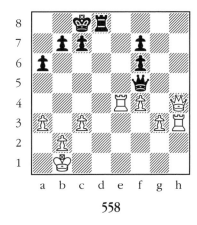

558

Saving a minor piece
Eliminate the attacker

Black to move.

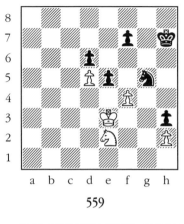

559

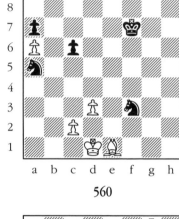

560

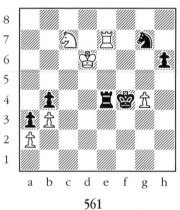

561

562

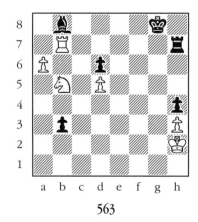

563

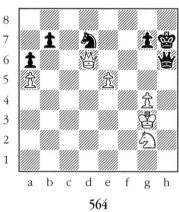

564

Get away from the attacked square

Black to move.

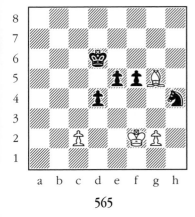

565

566

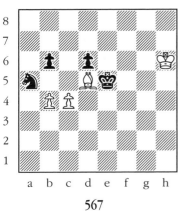

567

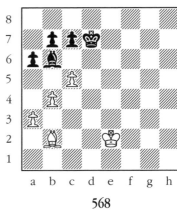

568

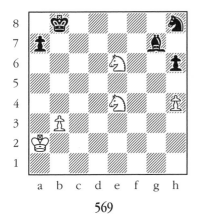

569

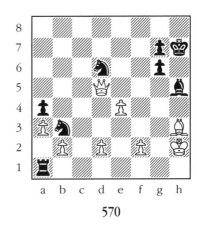

570

101

Block the attack

Black to move.

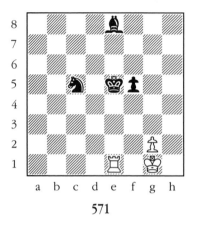

571

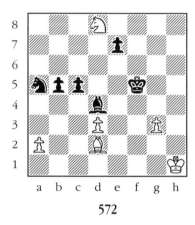

572

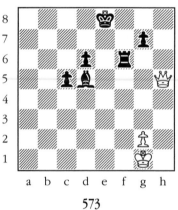

573

574

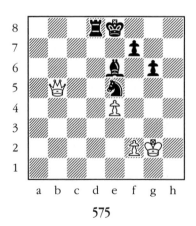

575

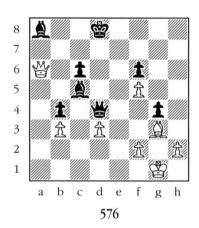

576

Counterattack

White to move.

577

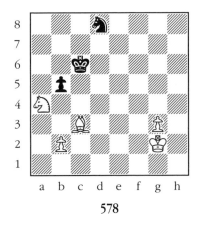

578

579

580

581

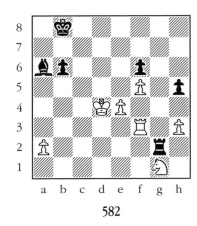

582

Defend with another piece or pawn

White to move.

583

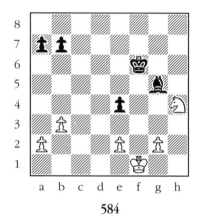

584

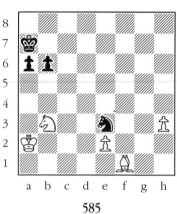

585

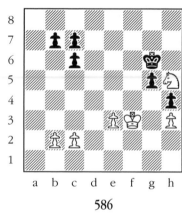

586

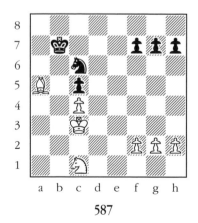

587

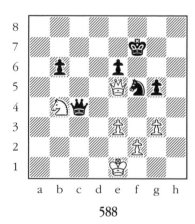

588

Pin

White to move.

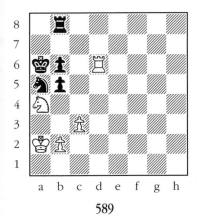

589

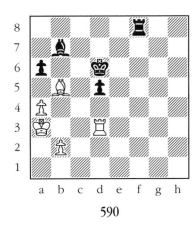

590

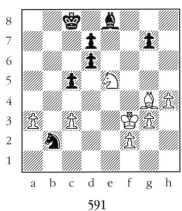

591

592

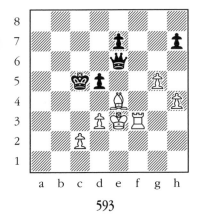

593

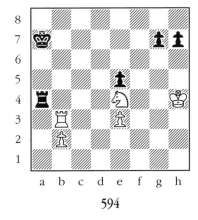

594

Practice
Attack or defense
Find the best move
White to move.

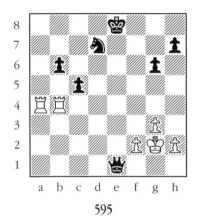

595

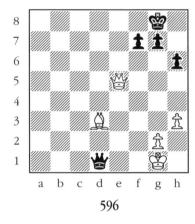

596

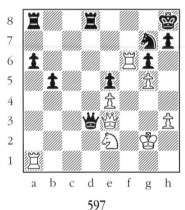

597

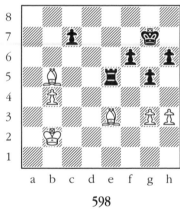

598

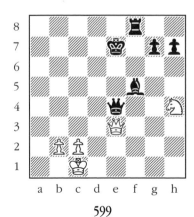

599

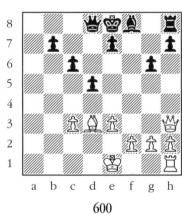

600

Find the best move

Black to move.

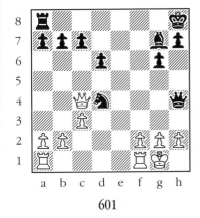

601

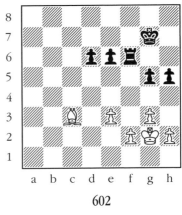

602

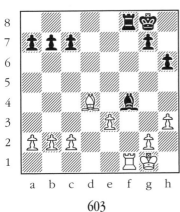

603

604

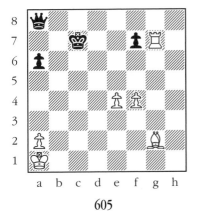

605

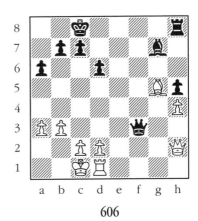

606

Find the best move

White to move.

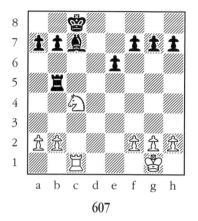

607

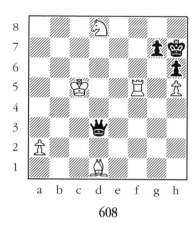

608

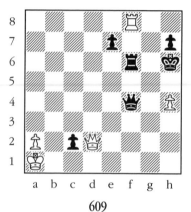

609

610

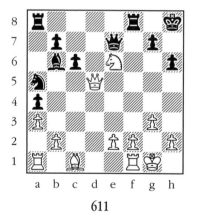

611

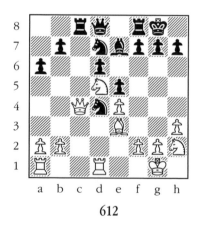

612

Find the best move

Black to move.

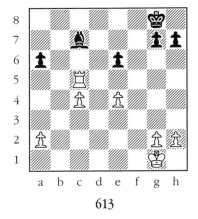

613

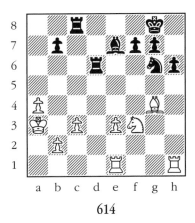

614

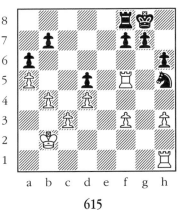

615

616

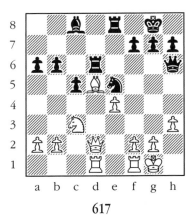

617

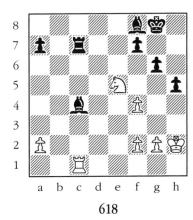

618

Solutions

1. 1...♖e8+.
2. 1...♖a4+.
3. 1...♗g7+.
4. 1...♗d4+.
5. 1...♕a5+.
6. 1...♕h1+.
7. 1. ♗xc6+.
8. 1. ♘xe6+.
9. 1. ♗xg7+.
10. 1. ♖xg7+.
11. 1. fxe6+.
12. 1. ♗xf6+.
13. 1. ♗xd3+.
14. 1. ♖h5+.
15. 1. ♘g7+.
16. 1. ♖d7+.
17. 1. ♘c7+.
18. 1. d7+.
19. 1. ♗c6++.
20. 1. ♘xd6++.
21. 1. bxc5++.
22. 1. ♘c4++.
23. 1. ♖e6++.
24. 1. ♘d5++.
25. 1. c5+.
26. 1. d6+.
27. 1. ♗b7+.
28. 1. ♖xb4+.
29. 1. ♗e5+.
30. 1. ♘c3+.
31. 1. e6+.
32. 1. f4+.
33. 1. ♗e3+.
34. 1. ♗d6+.
35. 1. ♘f6+.
36. 1. ♖xc5+.
37. 1. d7+.
38. 1. ♖h8+.
39. 1. ♗f6+.

40. 1. ♖d8+.
41. 1. ♖f8+.
42. 1. ♘f7+.
43. 1...♗b6+.
44. 1...♗xg2+.
45. 1...♘a2+.
46. 1...h2+.
47. 1...♖e6+.
48. 1...b3+.
49. 1. d7+.
50. 1. ♖a8+.
51. 1. ♗h7+.
52. 1. ♖xg6+.
53. 1. ♗a6+.
54. 1. ♗xe6+.
55. 1. ♖xe4+ ♔xe4 2. ♖e1+.
56. 1. ♖xf7+ ♔xf7 2. ♕h7+.
57. 1. ♖e5+ ♔xe5 2. ♕e3+.
58. 1. ♗xe5+ ♔xe5 2. ♕a1+.
59. 1. ♖xe5+ ♔xe5 2. ♕g5+.
60. 1. ♗xe3+ ♔xe3 2. ♕f2+.
61. 1. ♖xe6+ ♕xe6 2. d5+.
62. 1. ♖xe4+ ♕xe4 2. ♗xc6+.
63. 1. ♗b5+ ♔xb5 2. ♘xc7+.
64. 1. ♖xe4+ ♕xe4 2. ♘d6+.
65. 1. ♗xf7+ ♔xf7 (1...♕xf7 2. ♘d6+) 2. ♘e5+.
66. 1. ♗d7+ ♔xd7 (1...♕xd7 2. ♘f6+) 2. ♘e5+.
67. 1...♖a6+.

68. 1...♖e2+.
69. 1...♖h4+.
70. 1...♗d5+.
71. 1...♗xe6+.
72. 1...♗xf5+.
73. 1. ♖a6+.
74. 1. ♗xc6+.
75. 1. ♖xd7+.
76. 1. ♘xf6+.
77. 1. ♘d6+.
78. 1. ♕xa5+ and 2. ♕xc3.
79. 1...♖h1+ 2. ♔xh1 ♕xh3+.
80. 1...♗g2+ 2. ♔xg2 ♕xf4.
81. 1...g1♕+ 2. ♔xg1 ♕xa2.
82. 1...♗xb2+ 2. ♔xb2 ♕xa5.
83. 1...♖a1+ 2. ♔xa1 ♕xa3+.
84. 1...♗c3+ 2. ♔xc3 ♕xe3+.
85. 1. ♖h1+ ♔g8 2. ♕xg6.
86. 1. d7+ ♔f8 2. ♕xf6+.
87. 1. ♗h7+ ♕xh7 (1...♔h8 2. ♕xh6) 2. ♘xh7.
88. 1. ♘b5+ ♔a8 2. ♕xa6+.
89. 1. ♗e5+ ♔h7 2. ♕xg5.
90. 1. ♖h7+ ♔c8 2. ♕xd6.
91. 1. ♕h7+, and after 1...♔f8 there follows 2. ♕h8+.
92. 1. c4+, and Black can't avoid 2. ♗g3+.

93. 1. g6+ ♔h8 2. ♗g7+.
94. 1. b6+ ♔a8 2. b7+.
95. 1. ♖xe4+ fxe4 2. ♖xe4+.
96. 1. ♘xg6+ ♔g8 2. ♘xe7+.
97. 1. e7.
98. 1. ♗g6.
99. 1. ♗xc7.
100. 1. ♘e6.
101. 1. ♖a8.
102. 1. ♖g8.
103. 1...♗b3.
104. 1...♖f5.
105. 1...exd3.
106. 1...♗c5.
107. 1...♘c3.
108. 1...♘c4.
109. 1. ♗h6.
110. 1. ♗g8.
111. 1. ♔d7.
112. 1. ♖a5.
113. 1. ♔b7.
114. 1. ♘c6.
115. 1...♗b4.
116. 1...♖e8.
117. 1...♗h4.
118. 1...♗b4.
119. 1...♖a1.
120. 1...♗d4.
121. 1. ♖e8 ♕xe8 2. ♘c7+.
122. 1. ♗g5 ♕xg5 2. ♖xd5+.
123. 1. ♗b5 ♕xb5 2. ♘xc7+.
124. 1. ♗xh5 ♕xh5 2. ♘f6+.

110

125. 1. ♗xb5 ♕xb5 2. ♘c7+.

126. 1. ♖xe4 ♕xe4 2. ♗xg6+.

127. 1. c7.

128. 1. b7.

129. 1. ♗g2.

130. 1. ♗c7.

131. 1. ♖xb6 ♖xb6 (1...♘e7 2. ♖xc6+) 2. c8♕.

132. 1. ♗g5 ♕xg5 (1...♘e7 2. ♗xf6) 2. gxh8♕.

133. 1. f6 ♕xf6 (otherwise 2. ♕g7#) 2. ♖xf6.

134. 1. ♗f6 ♕g7 (White was threatening 2. ♖h8#) 2. ♗xg7.

135. 1. ♘c6 ♕xc6 (White was threatening 2. ♖xa7#) 2. bxc6.

136. 1. ♗c6 ♕xc6 (White was threatening 2. ♕xa6#) 2. dxc6.

137. 1. ♕g6 ♕f5 (White was threatening 2. ♕h7#, and if 1...gxf6, then 2. ♕xh6#) 2. ♕xf5.

138. 1. ♘g6 ♕xg6 (White was threatening 2. ♖h8#) 2. fxg6.

139. 1...♖c1+.

140. 1...♖b2+.

141. 1...♗e4+.

142. 1...♗b2+.

143. 1...♕g1+.

144. 1...♕h4+.

145. 1. ♗xe7+.

146. 1. cxd6+.

147. 1. ♕xb7+.

148. 1. ♘xf5+.

149. 1. ♗xg6+.

150. 1. ♘xg7+.

151. 1. d6+.

152. 1. ♗xd6+.

153. 1. ♘xc7+.

154. 1. ♘e7+.

155. 1. ♕g6+.

156. 1. ♕h5+.

157. 1...♘xc2++.

158. 1...♗b4++.

159. 1...♖c4++.

160. 1...♘b3++.

161. 1...♖h6++.

162. 1...♘e6++.

163. 1...♖xe2+.

164. 1...♖xf4+.

165. 1...♗b7+.

166. 1...♘g3+.

167. 1...♘e4+.

168. 1...e5+.

169. 1. e6+.

170. 1. d5+.

171. 1. e5+.

172. 1. f4+.

173. 1. axb5+.

174. 1. b4+.

175. 1. d7+.

176. 1. ♗f6+.

177. 1. ♖e8+.

178. 1. ♖b8+ ♖d8 (but not 1...♘e8 2. ♖xe8#) 2. ♖xd8+.

179. 1. ♖f5+.

180. 1. ♖g8+.

181. 1. e6+.

182. 1. e3+.

183. 1. ♗f7+.

184. 1. ♗a6+.

185. 1. ♘g5+.

186. 1. ♗c5+.

187. 1. ♖xa6+.

188. 1. ♕xg6+.

189. 1. ♘d5+.

190. 1. ♖xe6+.

191. 1. ♕b6+.

192. 1. ♕e5+.

193. 1...♕e5+ followed by 2...♖xe2.

194. 1...♕b5+.

195. 1...♕d7+.

196. 1...♕d6+.

197. 1...♖exe4+ and 2...♖xb4.

198. 1...♕d5+.

199. 1. d6+ ♔e8 2. d7+.

200. 1. ♖a7+ and 2. ♖a8+.

201. 1. ♗f7+ ♔h7 2. ♗g6+.

202. 1. ♘c7+ ♔a7 2. ♘b5+.

203. 1. ♕b5+ ♔a7 2. ♕b6+.

204. 1. ♕h5+ ♔e7 2. ♕e5+.

205. 1. ♔g1.

206. 1. g7.

207. 1. ♔b3.

208. 1. ♗b8.

209. 1. ♔f6.

210. 1. ♕c8.

211. 1...♗g7.

212. 1...♗c6.

213. 1...♗b2.

214. 1...♕g8.

215. 1...♕e4.

216. 1...♕a1 (but not 1...♕h8 2. h6).

217. 1...fxg3.

218. 1...cxb6.

219. 1...♕xf3.

220. 1...♗xc3.

221. 1...♗xf4.

222. 1...dxc4.

223. 1. d7.

224. 1. ♕d4.

225. 1. ♘f7.

226. 1. ♘f7.

227. 1. ♘xc7.

228. 1. ♘c6.

229. 1...c4.

230. 1...d5.

231. 1...b4.

232. 1...d3.

233. 1...g5.

234. 1...b4.

235. 1...b3.

236. 1...♖d4.

237. 1...♖xh4.

238. 1...c4.

239. 1...e4.

240. 1...♖f6.

241. 1. h7.

242. 1. ♔b5.

243. 1. d4.

244. 1. g7.

245. 1. g4.

246. 1. ♘c4.

247. 1...g5 followed by 2...♔g6.

248. 1...d6 followed by 2...♔b6.

249. 1...♖h8 with the idea of 2...♔b6.

250. 1...♔b5 followed by 2...♗e7.

251. 1...♘f6, and then 2...♔d2 and 3...♔e3.

252. 1...♗c1 with the idea of 2...♔d3 and 3...♔c2.

253. 1...♖xc2.

254. 1...♗b4.

255. 1...♗f8.

256. 1...♕h4.

257. 1...♖a2.

258. 1...♗a4.

111

259. 1. Rxh7 Rxh7 (White was threatening to take on f7) 2. Qxf8.

260. 1. Qd6.

261. 1. Qc5.

262. 1. Qe1.

263. 1. Qxf5.

264. 1. Qd1.

265. 1...Ke3 2. Kf1 (or 2. Rd3+ Kxd3) 2...Rh1+.

266. 1...Qb3 2. Rxd3 (Black threatened 2...Qc2#) 2...Q(R)xd3.

267. 1...Qg3 2. Rc1+ (Black threatened 2...Qh2#) 2...Bxc1.

268. 1...Nb4 2. Rd2 (Black threatened 2...Qxa2#) 2...Qxd2.

269. 1...Nc3 2. Ra4 (Black threatened 2...Rxa2#) 2...Nxa4.

270. 1...Ree1 2. Rg1 (defending against 2...Rh1#) 2...Rxg1.

271. 1...Ra1+.

272. 1...Bb2+.

273. 1...Rg6+.

274. 1...Bc6+.

275. 1...Qa3+.

276. 1...Qg1+.

277. 1. dxe5+.

278. 1. Rxb8+.

279. 1. Qxc8+.

280. 1. Rxh7+.

281. 1. Bxd7+.

282. 1. Rxh6+.

283. 1. f5+.

284. 1. Rc8+.

285. 1. Nf6+.

286. 1. Qd5+.

287. 1. Qh5+.

288. 1. Qa4+.

289. 1...Bxc3++.

290. 1...Nxd3++.

291. 1...Be5++.

292. 1...Rb5++.

293. 1...dxc4++.

294. 1...Nb5++.

295. 1. Bxb6+.

296. 1. Nxb6+.

297. 1. b6+.

298. 1. e4+.

299. 1. Nd4+.

300. 1. Bd4+.

301. 1. Bb6+.

302. 1...f3+.

303. 1...Ne5+.

304. 1...f5+.

305. 1...Ra7+.

306. 1...Nc5+.

307. 1...Re1+.

308. 1...Qa8+.

309. 1...Ra1+.

310. 1...Rg8+.

311. 1...Ra1+.

312. 1...c2+

313. 1. Nxe6+.

314. 1. Rxh6+.

315. 1. Qxb6+.

316. 1. Nf6+.

317. 1. Nc6+.

318. 1. Bxb7+.

319. 1. Qe4+.

320. 1. Qh6+.

321. 1. Qb2+.

322. 1. Qh1+.

323. 1. Qh8+.

324. 1. Qh1+.

325. 1. Rg1+ followed by 2. Rh1+.

326. 1. b4+ Ka6 2. b5+.

327. 1. Ng6+ Kh7 2. Nf8+.

328. 1. Rh8+ followed by 2. Ne5+.

329. 1. c4+ followed by 2. Ba3+.

330. 1. Bb5+ Kd8 2. Ne6+.

331. 1...c4.

332. 1...g5.

333. 1...Nc3.

334. 1...Kg2.

335. 1...Rb3.

336. 1...Qc3.

337. 1. Re1.

338. 1. Bg2.

339. 1. Rd7.

340. 1. f4.

341. 1. Ra6.

342. 1. Qh5.

343. 1. e5.

344. 1. Rd5.

345. 1. Rg4.

346. 1. Nc5.

347. 1. Ne5.

348. 1. Qa8.

349. 1. d5.

350. 1. Bb3.

351. 1. Nc5.

352. 1. a5.

353. 1. Nd6.

354. 1. Re4.

355. 1...Kh3.

356. 1...Be5.

357. 1...Nf3.

358. 1...Nd6.

359. 1...Rf1.

360. 1...Kc2.

361. 1. Nc5 followed by 2. Kc7.

362. 1. g3 followed by 2. Kg2.

363. 1. Nd2 followed by 2. Kb2.

364. 1. Ne3 followed by 2. Kh2.

365. 1. c4 followed by 2. b5.

366. 1. d3 followed by 2. Rb2.

367. 1. Rxb6.

368. 1. Qxg6.

369. 1. f4.

370. 1. h6.

371. 1. Qa1.

372. 1. Bc7 (but not 1. Bc5 Rb8).

373. 1. Qh1.

374. 1. Qd3.

375. 1. Bc2.

376. 1. Bc8.

377. 1. Qxc3.

378. 1. Qd1.

379. 1. Rf7+.

380. 1. Bf3+.

381. 1. Re8+.

382. 1. Qa2+.

383. 1. Qh7+.

384. 1. Qd7+.

385. 1...Rxg2+.

386. 1...Bxf3+.

387. 1...Qxd4+.

388. 1...dxe4+.

389. 1...Rxd3+.

390. 1...Bxb2+.

391. 1. Bb5+.

392. 1. Rxe4+.

393. 1. Bxf6+.

394. 1. Qa4+.

395. 1. Qh5+ (but not 1. Qa4+ c6).

396. 1. Qh8+.

397. 1...Rxd7+.

398. 1...Rxe3+.

399. 1...Rd5+.

400. 1...Nc8+.

401. 1...Be8+.

402. 1...♗a4+.

403. 1. d4+.

404. 1. ♘e5+.

405. 1. ♖e4+.

406. 1. d5+.

407. 1. ♗d5+.

408. 1. ♖b3+.

409. 1. h8♕+.

410. 1. ♖e1+.

411. 1. ♖d4+.

412. 1. ♗a6+.

413. 1. c7+.

414. 1. ♕d8+.

415. 1...♘xf3+.

416. 1...♖xh3+.

417. 1...♘xe4+.

418. 1...♗xc4+.

419. 1...♕xc3+.

420. 1...♘d4+.

421. 1. ♖d7.

422. 1. ♔f7.

423. 1. ♔f7.

424. 1. ♗f1.

425. 1. e5.

426. 1. ♕e5.

427. 1...♖d3.

428. 1...♗g6.

429. 1...♕e8.

430. 1...♗c6.

431. 1...♖f5.

432. 1...♕a8.

433. 1...e5.

434. 1...♖d6.

435. 1...♗d5.

436. 1...♖f4.

437. 1...♗c5.

438. 1...♕d4.

439. 1...c4.

440. 1...g4.

441. 1...♗e3.

442. 1...c5.

443. 1...♗e6.

444. 1...♘e6.

445. 1...b4 followed by 2...♔c2.

446. 1...♗e5 followed by 2...♔g6.

447. 1...h4 followed by 2...f5.

448. 1...♘c5 followed by 2...♔g7.

449. 1...♖d4 followed by 2...c3.

450. 1...f6 followed by 2...♔f7 and 3...♔g7.

451. 1...e5.

452. 1...c5.

453. 1...♗b7.

454. 1...e4.

455. 1...♕a5.

456. 1...♕e7.

457. 1...♔xe7.

458. 1...♘xf6.

459. 1...♘xc7.

460. 1...♖xg6.

461. 1...♗xa6.

462. 1...♗xh8.

463. 1. ♔e3.

464. 1. ♔f3.

465. 1. ♔f4.

466. 1. ♔f1.

467. 1. ♔d4.

468. 1. ♔g3.

469. 1. f6.

470. 1. ♘f5+.

471. 1. ♘b4.

472. 1. ♘d3.

473. 1. ♗b6.

474. 1. ♕g7.

475. 1...exf4.

476. 1...♗xe1.

477. 1...♔b7.

478. 1...♔d6.

479. 1...♘f5.

480. 1...♖g8.

481. 1. ♗xf8.

482. 1. ♗xc6.

483. 1. ♕xe8.

484. 1. ♕xe8+.

485. 1. ♕xd8, and White's d-pawn queens.

486. 1. ♕xe8+ ♕xe8 2. ♖f8, winning back the queen.

487. 1. ♕d6.

488. 1. ♕g4.

489. 1. ♕h6.

490. 1. ♕xa7.

491. 1. ♕a6.

492. 1. ♕d8.

493. 1...♖h5.

494. 1...♘e7.

495. 1...♘d5.

496. 1...♗b5.

497. 1...b5.

498. 1...e5.

499. 1...♗xb1+.

500. 1...♗h4+.

501. 1...♖a6.

502. 1...♗e4.

503. 1...♗d7.

504. 1...♘d5.

505. 1. ♕xb2+ ♖xb2, stalemate.

506. 1. ♕xh5+ ♕xh5, stalemate.

507. 1. ♔a3 ♖xc2, stalemate.

508. 1. ♔h1 ♗xf2, stalemate.

509. 1. ♔c2 ♖xd4, stalemate.

510. 1. ♕h2+ ♗xh2, stalemate.

511. 1...♘g3+ (but not 1...♕xa8, because of the in-between check 2. ♘f3+) 2. ♔h2 ♘f1+, perpetual check.

512. 1...♗c2+ 2. ♔a2 ♗b3+, perpetual check.

513. 1...♖g2+ 2. ♔h1 ♖g1+, perpetual check.

514. 1...♘c3+ 2. ♔c1 (but not 2. ♔a1 ♖a2#) 2...♘a2+, perpetual check.

515. 1...♗xe5+ 2. ♔g1 ♗d4+, perpetual check.

516. 1...♘g2+ and then 2...♘e3+, with perpetual check.

517. 1. ♕xb5.

518. 1. ♕xb6.

519. 1. ♕xh6.

520. 1. ♗xc4.

521. 1. ♖d1.

522. 1. ♖d2.

523. 1. ♖d1, and Black can't play 1...♖xa1 because of 2. ♖d8#.

524. 1. ♖a1, and Black can't play 1...♗xh3 because of 2. ♖a8#.

525. 1. ♘f6, and because of the threat of 2. ♖h7#, Black has to play 1...♗e4.

526. 1. ♗h6, and Black can't play 1...exd1♕ because of 2. ♗g7#.

527. 1. ♘e5, and Black can't play 1...♘xh4 because of 2. ♘f7#.

113

528. 1. ♗e2, and Black can't play 1... ♗xh6 because of 2. ♗a6#.

529. 1... ♖f7.

530. 1... ♖d7.

531. 1... ♖b7.

532. 1... ♖d6 (but not 1... ♖d7 2. ♕e6+).

533. 1... ♖a4 (but not 1... ♖d5 or 1... ♖e4, because of 2. ♗f3).

534. 1... ♖c7 (the only move, since Black has to watch out for 2. ♘e7+, which could follow after the careless 1... ♖xf5).

535. 1. ♖f3.

536. 1. d4.

537. 1. ♖e3.

538. 1.♘f3.

539. 1. d5.

540. 1. ♗b2.

541. 1...♘d4+.

542. 1...b5+.

543. 1...e5+.

544. 1...♗a2.

545. 1...♘d7.

546. 1...♘gf6.

547. 1...♗e5.

548. 1...♔f6.

549. 1...♕d4.

550. 1...♘f5.

551. 1...♖c7.

552. 1...f6.

553. 1. ♗e3.

554. 1. ♗b4.

555. 1. ♖b4.

556. 1. ♖xd4.

557. 1. ♕g4.

558. 1. ♕h7.

559. 1...exf4+.

560. 1...♘xe1.

561. 1... ♖xe7.

562. 1...♗xc4+.

563. 1... ♖xb7.

564. 1...♕xd6.

565. 1...♘g6.

566. 1...♘g5.

567. 1...♘b3.

568. 1...♗a7.

569. 1...♗e5.

570. 1...♘e8.

571. 1...♘e4.

572. 1...b4.

573. 1...♗f7.

574. 1...♗d7.

575. 1...♘d7.

576. 1...♗a7.

577. 1. ♔f7.

578. 1. ♗f6.

579. 1. ♘e5.

580. 1. ♘e6.

581. 1. g4.

582. 1. ♖a3.

583. 1. b4.

584. 1. g3.

585. 1. ♘d2.

586. 1. ♔g4.

587. 1. ♘b3.

588. 1. ♕b2.

589. 1. ♘c5+.

590. 1. ♗c4.

591. 1. ♘c6.

592. 1. ♗e6.

593. 1. ♖f5.

594. 1. ♖a3.

595. 1. ♖e4+, and White wins the queen for a rook.

596. 1. ♗f1, saving the bishop.

597. 1. ♖f8+, winning the queen for a rook.

598. 1. ♗c5, saving the bishops.

599. 1. ♘xf5+, winning the queen.

600. 1. ♗xg6+, winning the exchange.

601. 1...♘f3+, winning White's queen for the knight.

602. 1...e5, getting rid of the pin.

603. 1...♗h2+, winning the exchange.

604. 1...♗a6, and White has to give up either a bishop, or the queen for two minor pieces.

605. 1...♕h8, and White loses the rook due to the pin.

606. 1...♗b2+, winning the exchange.

607. 1. ♘d6+, winning the rook.

608. 1. ♖d5, defending both minor pieces.

609. 1. ♖xf6+, winning the queen (but not 1. ♕xf4+ ♖xf4 2. ♖xf4 c1♕#).

610. 1. ♗b5+, winning the queen for a bishop.

611. 1. ♘xf8, winning an exchange, because after 1...cxd5 White plays 2. ♘g6+ and 3. ♘xe7.

612. 1. ♕xc8, and Black loses a rook.

613. 1...♗b6, winning the rook.

614. 1...♖d4+, and discovered check wins the bishop.

615. 1...♘g3, winning a rook.

616. 1...♖c2, and the pin allows Black to save both pieces.

617. 1...♘f3+, winning the queen because 2. gxf3 leads to checkmate after, for example, 2...♖g6+ 3. ♔h2 ♕xh3#.

618. 1...♗d6 allows Black to keep the extra piece, since White can't play 2. ♘xc4 ♗xf4+, while 2. ♖xc4 is answered strongly by 2...♗xe5.